Taiwan—A Light in the East

David Pendery

Taiwan—A Light in the East

A Personal and Analytical Taiwan Study

palgrave
macmillan

David Pendery
National Taipei University of Business
Taipei, Taiwan

ISBN 978-981-15-5603-6 ISBN 978-981-15-5604-3 (eBook)
https://doi.org/10.1007/978-981-15-5604-3

This Palgrave Macmillan imprint is published by the registered company Springer Nature Singapore Pte Ltd.
The registered company address is: 152 Beach Road, #21-01/04 Gateway East, Singapore 189721, Singapore

No acknowledgments are stated here. The work is entirely the work of the author, with no co-authors.

For Taiwan and the Taiwanese, a land and people I love.
For my wife Hope, who helps me so much.
For my mother, "the branch does not fall far from the tree."

Included Works

1. "Taiwanese settling far and wide: a global view," *Taipei Times*, February 2, 2018
2. "Good things happening in Taiwan," *Taipei Times*, March 9, 2018
3. "New Approach to diplomatic bind," *Taipei Times*, October 8, 2019
4. "NAM is not a solution for Taiwan," *Taipei Times*, August 24, 2019
5. "Taiwan's own Meiji Restoration: A Chance for Peaceful Resolutions to Potential Crises," *Taiwan News*, September 13, 2019
6. "A chance at peace across the Strait," *Taipei Times*, June 13, 2019
7. "Taiwanese independence: it's in the air," *Taipei Times*, November 9, 2017
8. "Free discussion on independence," *Taipei Times*, February 15, 2019
9. "Donald Trump, Taiwan and China," *Taipei Times*, October 26, 2017
10. "Taiwan and the UN: A castle in air," *Taipei Times*, October 13, 2017
11. "Building consensuses old and new," *Taipei Times*, October 19, 2018
12. "Taiwan threatened by myriad risks," *Taipei Times*, June 6, 2018
13. "New award needed to honor allies," *Taipei Times*, 2020
14. "Teaching Philosophy and Methods," unpublished
15. "The Dao of Teaching," excerpt, unpublished
16. "Taiwanese students not so happy," *Taipei Times*, October 20, 1014
17. "Taiwan could be a leader in well-being," *Taipei Times*, January 14, 2020
18. "Taiwan a 'city on a hill' for Asia," *Taipei Times*, April 2, 2019
19. "On being a foreigner in Taiwan," *Taipei Times*, January 3, 2018

20. "Tombs are not for the dead," *Taipei Times*, May 17, 2015
21. "Taiwan is a true transnational state," *Taipei Times*, July 3, 2019
22. "Solidarity worldwide crucial at this time," *Taipei Times*, April 14, 2020 23. "Outbreaks need order, not protests," *Taipei Times*, May 1, 2020

Foreword

I was very honored when David Pendery approached me in November 2019 and asked for an interview on his book project on Taiwan history, politics, life, culture, education, identity, and the future prospects in Taiwan.

At that time, I had just left Taiwan after one decade of teaching and research on the island, and I remained deeply involved with Taiwan Studies as an associate fellow at the European Research Center on Contemporary Taiwan—A CCK Foundation Overseas Center (CCKF-ERCCT) at Eberhard Karls Universität Tübingen, Germany. I am also a board member and founding member of the European Association of Taiwan Studies. I feel a deep commitment to the island, having friends and colleagues in Taipei, Kaohsiung, and Taiwan, and many other associates working on Taiwan in academia all over the world.

When David approached me, I wondered how he would deal with his task, as it seemed that he wanted to cover all aspects of history and life in Taiwan. Later I realized that David was also an editorial writer for the *Taipei Times*, the only English newspaper with a print edition in Taiwan, and that he was not writing a multi-volume work covering all the above-mentioned topics, but had chosen more a essayistic/feuilletonist approach to Taiwan, based on his experience, and also his teaching and various writings, both academically and for the newspaper. I then became even more fascinated, having taught various courses on modern Taiwanese history, nationalism, gender, and civil society in Taiwan and other "Chinese societies" around the world. David describes his own journey to "becoming Taiwanese," in his first Taiwan book, *Something Super: Living, Learning and Teaching in Taiwan*, and yet more meticulously in this book, *Taiwan: A Light in the East, A Personal and Analytical Taiwan Study.*

This book covers the impressive uniqueness of Taiwan, the nation's vibrant society that emerged after the lifting of Martial Law in 1987, the island's struggles with its past and its colonial history, and its unique current geopolitical situation. These are dealt with carefully in the chapters "Taiwan: History, Politics and Culture" and "Identity: Being Taiwanese."

In various chapters David discusses the Gordian knot of identity politics in Taiwan, and the sovereignty question, which is linked to the dominant one-China policy and also to the fact that, unlike other parts of the world striving for independence, Taiwan is in almost all aspects in no way controlled by Beijing, which gives the island a much larger leeway to develop its own path—although admittedly the final outcome is unknown. David lets readers take part in his well-articulated thoughts, describing the likelihoods, contingencies, and the risks presented to the island.

But there is another aspect which makes the book worth reading: his personal involvement, his "becoming Taiwanese" himself, his fascination and love for the island. All of this complexity and elaboration has not blinded David to the real problems facing Taiwan, not least the nation's quest for an independent identity, its chaotic political situation, and these days dealing with the coronavirus epidemic. But at the same time he describes more commonplace problems, such as when foreigners attempt to become an integral part of society merely by obtaining a drivers' licenses, or the challenges of actually becoming an ROC citizen.

More of David's analysis deals with education in Taiwan. Having taught on the island for a decade, I feel with David when he describes the atmosphere in the universities, which still need improvement to encourage students to be more creative and not be bound by old Confucian traditions or the hierarchical bureaucracy of the ministry of education.

I highly recommend this book for everybody living on the island and interested in Taiwan in general. Taiwanese who are fluent in English will see their beautiful island through the eyes of a foreigner who has fallen in love with the island. In addition, I think those academically interested in Asia and East Asia should have a look at this book and find similarities and differences when comparing the history, society, and the personal life of a foreigner in nations in this part of the world—whether Taiwan, South Korea, Thailand, Malaysia, Mainland China, Hong Kong, Macau, or Singapore. Enjoy this excellent work examining these fascinating topics.

Non-resident Associate Fellow at the European
Research Center on Contemporary Taiwan, Eberhard
Karls Universität Tübingen, Tübingen, Germany
May 2020 Jens Damm

Contents

About the Author

David Pendery was born in Cincinnati, Ohio, on July 3, 1960, the Year of the Rat in Chinese culture. He grew up in Albuquerque, New Mexico. He dropped out of college when he was 18 and began a career as an electrician, and later as a fire alarm technician. He moved to San Francisco when he was 24 and worked in various jobs and occasionally as a musician. In 1990, he returned to college at the City College of San Francisco and then transferred to San Francisco State University, where he received his bachelor's degree in International Relations in 1995. In 1996, he moved to Massachusetts to attend Boston University, where he received a master's degree in Journalism in 1997. He then worked as a journalist and technical writer. In 2000 he relocated to Taiwan, where he began his career as an editor, English Consultant, and teacher of English. He attended National Chengchi University and received his PhD in English Literature and Historiography in 2010. He is now an associate professor at National Taipei University of Business. He is married to a Taiwanese woman and they have a 4-year-old daughter, Ariadne.

Pendery has published four books to date, including *"Hir'd or Coerc'd": The Creation of Narrative Historical Writing*, *Read All About It! Course and Material Design for Active ESP Journalism and News English Teaching*, *Wings of Knowledge: Western Literature for College Students*, and *Chaos and Old Night: Academic Works of David Pendery*. He has published editorials and commentary extensively in the English-language *Taipei Times* newspaper and in other periodicals.

List of Figures

CHAPTER 1

Introduction

As an expatriate living in Taiwan, a nation seen by some as a heart of Asia, I have experienced many amazing experiences that have bridged cultures, languages, education, politics, attitudes, behavior, identity, and the views and chronicles of varied peoples. Looking across Taiwan's history, with its mostly unknown origins, to the 1600s when the colonial eras began, to control under the Chinese Qing dynasty in the nineteenth century, to the short-lived Republic of Formosa in 1895, to the Japanese colonial dominion from 1895 to 1945, to the Chinese Nationalist Party (Kuomintang, KMT) authoritarian era from 1949 to 1987, and to the nation's breakthrough into a free, democratic republic after the 1980s—Taiwan, a "light in the East," is an amazing multicultural country, a rich and varied polity, which has much to offer in terms of politics, culture, history, aesthetics, esprit de corps, learning, literacy, identity, and being.

As a foreigner, I have unique roles to play in Taiwan, and my life has been steeped in culture shock, linguistic challenges, and cultural wonders, for many years. To make a long story short, I arrived in Taiwan in 2000, with few prospects in front of me, but things picked up fast. I found a job working as a teacher at a prominent national university, and after a short stint at a (notorious) "cram school," I began working full-time as an English consultant in a major international organization. From there I taught as a full-time instructor at another well-known university. Not long after this I married a Taiwanese woman, and my life in Taiwan began in earnest, taking exciting and enjoyable new turns (our daughter was born

D. Pendery, *Taiwan—A Light in the East*,
https://doi.org/10.1007/978-981-15-5604-3_1

in 2016, a wondrous experience, but I will not convey these details here). I entered a doctoral program in 2004, and from that time worked part-time at various teaching and tutoring jobs until 2010, when I received my PhD. From there I obtained full-time positions as a professor in universities, culminating in my current position as an associate professor at National Taipei University of Business (NTUB). During all of this time I have studied Chinese and other subjects assiduously; spent a lot of time playing my favorite game, tennis; practiced my long-time love of guitar and music; spent many enjoyable vacations and trips traveling everywhere in Taiwan (as well as a number of vacations to France, Hong Kong, Macau, Japan, and the United States); and enjoyed life in many other marvelous ways.

The above is a brief introduction to my life in Taiwan. I have told my story in my memoir, *Something Super: Living, Learning and Teaching in Taiwan* (Lynx Publishing, 2013). I refer readers to this work for a complete and detailed account of the life of a foreigner in Taiwan. I will refer to this work in this book, but not often, for as noted this book is not a personal story and is instead an analytical and diagnostic view of Taiwan's politics, culture, life, history, education, aesthetics, and individuality (the principal section from my memoir that I will relate is an adapted examination of independence in Taiwan).

This work is in many ways a "political" and/or analytical examination, and to be sure the politics and civic life of Taiwan are looked at broadly and critically. In a word, although I have some personal views, this is not a personal story. On this note, I add that as a long-term resident of Taiwan, I have interacted in any number of personal ways with dozens and dozens of people, and I have in turn developed a personal attachment here. Thus, even when I am writing analytical essays for publication in local newspapers, I have a bit of personal connection in the background. I do not think this can be avoided, but most importantly I do not think it results in any sort of bias, and my essays and other remarks remain just that: impartial, fair-minded, wholly analytical, non-partisan commentary.

Rather than the private and individual, this book takes up the more public interests I have had for many years. I was always a "political animal" in my life in the United States, and as far back as Richard Nixon I have closely studied and scrutinized political life and figures. I never missed a vote in the United States from the time I was 18, all the way up to my life in Taiwan, where I have submitted absentee ballot votes in presidential elections. I was always up for a political discussion about current issues, from my youngest years. My study of International Relations at San Francisco State University was something of the culmination of these interests. To be perfectly frank I was always seen as a firm liberal, in opposition to what I saw as stark, uncompromising, hard-nosed, essentially ungenerous Republican/conservative views (and oh my opposition was firm). I cannot take such a stance in Taiwan, as here there is not the same glaring difference in terms of opinions of the two main political parties, the "Blue" KMT and the ostensibly more "liberal" Democratic Progressive Party (the "Green" DPP). I will examine this conception and my views of the two political parties in Taiwan below.

I relate my diagnostic studies of Taiwan life in this book principally by way of editorials I have written for the largest English-language newspaper in Taiwan, the *Taipei Times*, as well as in other works (including letters to this newspaper). Each chapter in *Taiwan: A Light in the East* will include an introductions and additional analyses of the seven main chapters, leading to the inclusion of these published works. All of this is followed with a conclusion. This work may take part in a "golden age of Taiwan studies," as has been said by others, examining Taiwan's social, political, and cultural transformation and identification within and without its borders. To be sure there are Taiwan studies groups and institutes at universities and other institutions worldwide, and if this is true, I look forward to participating in such examinations. Former Taiwanese President Ma Ying-jeou (馬英九) proposed establishing a Taiwan Academy educational system around the world in order to apprise the international community of Taiwan's culture and development and promote Mandarin learning (using traditional Chinese characters, as opposed to the simplified system used in China), Sinology studies, and the study of Taiwan's diverse cultures. I always liked this idea (I am not objecting to China's Confucius Institutes, but feel that such an approach on this side of the Taiwan Strait makes perfect sense). Planning and implementation has been handled by the Ministry of Culture and other groups in Taiwan, but it has not been launched yet.

I should say however that some would see my stances and opinions as restricted, because my Chinese skills are not advanced enough that I can read political news in every newspaper and understand every statement that politicians make. This is no doubt true, but the local English newspaper, the *Taipei Times*, and many other international newspapers and wire services cover Taiwan news and politics very attentively. So, I can in effect keep up on the news effectively.

Overall in this work, I hope to create a systematic, relevant, and in essence scholarly (if somewhat easygoing and personal) study of important issues and topics in Taiwan, which I think many readers will be interested in, including academic professionals interested in international affairs in general and Taiwan studies particularly; those interested in the nation's relationship with China, the United States, and other nations and entities; and students of Taiwan studies proper—the nation's politics, culture, history, life, education, peoples, aesthetics, and identity. As well, I think many tourists and visitors in Taiwan will enjoy the book, as will English-speaking citizens and long-term foreign residents in Taiwan and other Asian countries. Let us begin our study of this fascinating "island in the stream."

CHAPTER 2

Taiwan: History, Politics, and Culture

To begin, let me turn to Taiwan's history. Admittedly, before the 1600s, not much is known about this nation. It is known that people have lived here for 20,000–30,000 years, and bone fragments and various artifacts have been unearthed and can be seen in museums in Taiwan. In spite of such archeological finds, however, not a lot is known in terms of Taiwan's early history. There is, however, one fascinating probability that is being examined by scientists, linguists, and anthropologists. This is the "out of Taiwan" thesis, which indicates that the ancestries and disbursement of nations and empires in the Austronesian area may have originated with the odysseys of peoples from Taiwan. Evidence has shown that "Pacific populations originated in Taiwan around 5200 years ago," and migration from Taiwan "played a major role in the spread of people throughout the world" (*Science Daily*, Jan. 27, 2009). This possible source of Austronesian peoples and their great civilizations is compelling and is probably at least in part true (although the possibility that Austronesia was founded by peoples from China or other Asian nations is also a probable likelihood). This theory was originated by linguist Robert Blust (currently professor in the Department of Linguistics at the University of Hawai'i at Manoa) and later voiced from an archaeological perspective by Professor Peter Bellwood (emeritus professor of archaeology at the School of Archaeology and Anthropology of the Australian National University). I find this theory fascinating, in that it indicates how the Taiwanese are a diasporic people, settling far and wide, inhabiting new regions and founding new nations

D. Pendery, *Taiwan—A Light in the East*,
https://doi.org/10.1007/978-981-15-5604-3_2

and even empires (Fig. 2.1). This can also be seen in recent Taiwanese history, with Taiwanese settling in and creating new communities in many areas around the world (part of the "Chinese diaspora"). With this idea in mind, I would like to introduce the first of my published works, "Taiwanese settling far and wide: A global view," published in the *Taipei Times* on February 5, 2018. I view this actuality from the standpoint of Taiwanese identity, mindfulness, and consciousness and even call the modern movements of Taiwanese peoples my own "out of Taiwan" thesis. Much of this examination looks at how "diaspora is a powerful challenge to the hegemony and boundedness of the nation-state and any pure imaginary of nationhood" (Wang, 28), suggesting how leaving and breaking out of one's "bounds" relieves feelings of "boundedness." If all of this is true, we

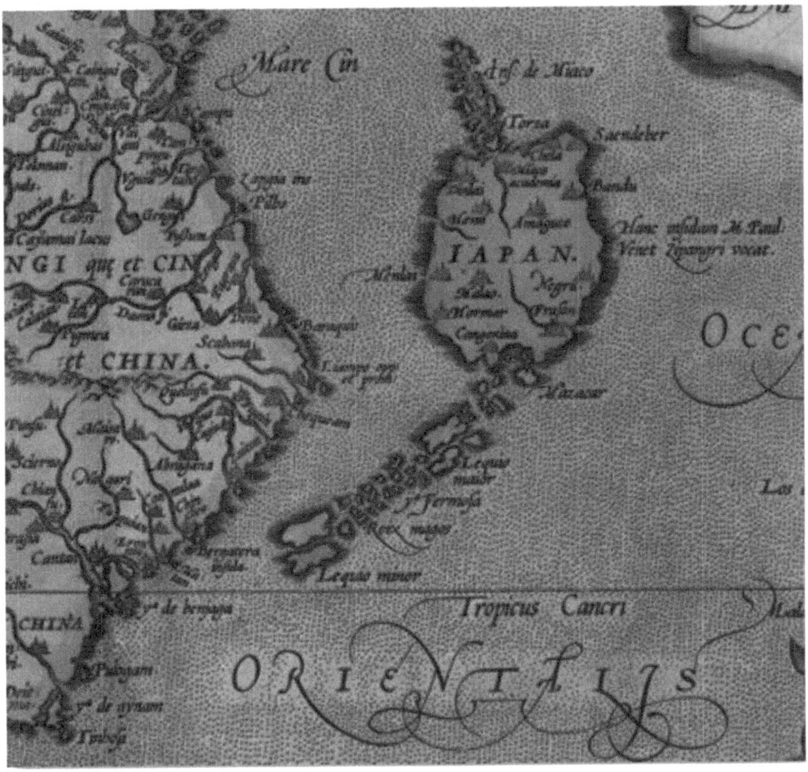

Fig. 2.1 Sixteenth-century map of Taiwan

may see that Taiwan has contributed to the modern world in important developmental ways.

Taiwanese Settling Far and Wide: A Global View

This piece is in response to Jerome Keating's "Taiwan's great epic of migration" in the February 1 *Taipei Times*. Keating hales the possibility of an "out of Taiwan" thesis, which can explain the origins and settlement of nations and empires in the Austronesian region, an idea that has a prominent following in scientific circles. This "epic" understanding of the source of Austronesian peoples is compelling and is probably at least in part true, but the possibility that Austronesia was founded by peoples from China or other Southeast Asian nations, which had ancient seafaring peoples who also voyaged into these regions, is also a distinct likelihood. The actual origins of Austronesia peoples, ethnicities, and languages are not fully understood at this time, unlike, for example, the diaspora from Russia and China that crossed the Bering Strait into North and then to South America, or the out of Africa thesis explaining the origins of almost all of mankind. For these reasons, it is not appropriate to claim the origin of Austronesia as Taiwan's own, at least not yet.

Though looking at ancient exodus and the origins it gave rise to is interesting, and will no doubt cast light on Taiwan's rich past, and help solidify and amalgamate Taiwanese identity, I think a different look might be even more compelling. This is a look at Taiwan's recent past, comprising another great migration that is just as interesting and relevant. Here I mean the diaspora out of Taiwan since World War II and the significant impact that has had around the world. It could be said that this is related to the Chinese Diaspora, which has been occurring since the mid-1900s—and indeed the migration of Taiwanese peoples to other lands has been going on for almost as long. But let's look at Taiwan in more modern times. In the modern age, Taiwanese people have in a sense found a new identity in their migrations, which coheres in important ways in the contemporary world.

Taiwanese students are in some senses at the core of this migration. They have been travelling to other countries in great numbers for the last 70 years. Taiwanese students have been studying widely in the United States since the 1950s, long before Chinese students began to study there in larger numbers, and these and other Taiwanese have been called a "first wave" of immigration to America. More recently, a superfluous number of

Taiwanese students study in the United States (approximately 25,000), and it has been said that Taiwanese Americans have the highest educational attainment rank in the United States, surpassing any other ethnic group or country. (In contrast, there were about 19,000 Taiwanese studying in Europe in 2013–2014, most of whom were in the United Kingdom; there were 7200 in Australia.)

By the same token, ordinary Taiwanese citizens have also been migrating to the United States. There were 196,691 Taiwanese in the United States in the 2010 census (and many more of Taiwanese descent). This is much less than the 3,137,061 Chinese, but by no means insignificant. And as well, Taiwanese students, working professionals, and families have been migrating to other nations around the world for almost as long, again reflecting the global perspective of Taiwanese migration. I do not consider this a "narrow perspective" as Keating states. It is truly a global view, with Taiwanese people migrating and settling far and wide.

If the "out of Taiwan" thesis proves to be true, the modern diaspora, with its hundreds and thousands of people, may never match the empires and nations that were given rise to in ancient times. But it may be no less important to Taiwanese identity and consciousness. With Taiwan having shaped the modern world in significant ways, giving so much back, this may one day comprise an epic of its own. As with Keating, I hope this story is one day told. Telling stories is sharing stories; sharing stories is bolstering the quality of life and experience. This is what we look forward to.

To return to the history of Taiwan proper, the Dutch East India Company settled here in 1623 (the Portuguese had already dubbed Taiwan *Ilha Formosa*, the beautiful island, in the 1500s, but they were unable to establish themselves on the island). The Dutch constructed Fort Zeelandia as a trading base between Japan and China, and this fortress can still be seen in Tainan in southern Taiwan (Fig. 2.2). They built other edifices and set out to turn Taiwan into a Dutch colony. They were strict and often violent with the aboriginal people and, at their worst, "the Dutch were racist, abused human rights, and indulged in slavery" (Jacobs, no page number). The Dutch set up a tax system and opened schools to teach a romanized version of aboriginal languages, as well as the Dutch language. Such instruction in non-native languages became common in Taiwan during various colonial eras, up until Japanese rule from 1895 to 1945 (and for that matter, after). After 1949, standard Chinese Mandarin was emphasized in Taiwanese schools, with the authoritarian KMT government

Fig. 2.2 Fort Zeelandia by J. Vingboons, circa 1635

punishing those who spoke and taught local and aboriginal languages. Many of these dialects in turn went into decline from 1949 on, although this trend has been reversed in the modern era. Professor Jens Damm writes that Taiwan now "[allows] and [promotes] the use of various languages and dialects, and [protects] the rights of the Aborigines" (Damm, 2012, 85). Taiwan's native peoples have 42 dialects and 16 officially recognized languages, and an act has been passed to preserve them. Taiwan's Council of Indigenous Peoples aims to promote "quality of life among indigenous peoples…to enhance the living standards of the pride among indigenous tribes and to restore their confidence and status" (Council of Indigenous Peoples website).

Additionally, Christianity was evangelized during the Dutch era and forced on the local peoples (in some senses to this day Christianity is a relatively common belief in Taiwan). Dutch control was primarily limited to the western plain in the south of the island. At almost this same time, the Spanish Empire established a settlement on the northeast coast of Taiwan. The Spanish built Fort San Domingo in 1629, but abandoned this structure by 1638 (the British later took it up as one of their consulates in Taiwan, and it can still be seen in Tamsui [actual spelling Danshui]; Fig. 2.3). In 1642, the Dutch ejected the Spanish from the north of the island, while they themselves were driven out by Koxinga (國姓爺, actual

Fig. 2.3 The former British consular residence and Fort San Domingo

pronunciation Guo Xing-ye), a loyalist Ming strongman, in 1662. This ended the early period of colonial control in Taiwan, and after this, the Qing Chinese Empire nominally ruled the country, but they never put much into this. In 1860, after the Second Opium War, the unequal Treaty of Peking forced the Qing dynasty to open up Taiwanese ports in Kaohsiung, Anping, Tamsui, and Keelung to foreign trade. At this time, the United Kingdom established a consulate in Kaohsiung in the south, as well as in the former Spanish Fort San Domingo in the north of Taiwan. Though Britain was never truly a colonial power in Taiwan, the presence of Westerners played an important role in life here for a long time thereafter. France made a small, unsuccessful attempt to make claims in Taiwan in the late 1800s. It was after this, with the Treaty of Shimonoseki concluding the first Sino-Japanese war in 1895, that Taiwan was ceded to Japan, control which it would have until 1945. Japan became the most prominent and important of all the colonial powers in Taiwan: developing the infrastructure on the island in important ways; conducting extensive scientific research on the environment, flora, and fauna; introducing Japanese education and language across the island (many elderly Taiwanese can still speak Japanese); and attempting to integrate the population into the Japanese Empire (one aspect of this was that many young Taiwanese men were forced to fight with the Japanese during World War II). As with other colonial powers, conflict with the local peoples was often serious. One of the most important conflicts was the Seediq rebellion, which saw the Seediq people launch a number of attacks, including an assault on a village in which many Japanese politicians and law enforcement personnel were meeting in 1930, killing over 130 Japanese. In response, the Japanese launched a ruthless counter-attack, killing over 600 Seediq. This is known as the Wushe Incident and was featured in the popular 2011 film, *Seediq Bale*. Such incidents were relatively common in Taiwan, although at the same time the Japanese and Taiwanese in many ways got along reasonably well and cooperated. To this day, many Taiwanese do not resent what the Japanese did and see the positive development they engendered as important (the Taiwan rail system, a key part of life and transportation here, was almost entirely developed by the Japanese; to be sure Taiwanese people have continued such development to the present day, culminating in the extraordinary Taipei MRT subway system and the just-as-extraordinary High Speed Rail from the north to south; Fig. 2.4). However, many Taiwanese intellectuals and cultural leaders were suppressed by the Japanese, which is seen in a negative light.

Fig. 2.4 Taiwan rail

We might observe here that some people view the transitions from Dutch to Spanish to Japanese rule (with a few other nations tossed in for good measure), as the origin of that which is multicultural about Taiwan. This is not really accurate. After all, few people in Taiwan speak Dutch or Spanish (outside of a few students studying the languages), and only a handful of elderly people speak Japanese. Although Japan did leave a strong mark on Taiwan (the two nations are in some senses like siblings to this day), these other nations did not leave truly significant traditions, institutions, or cultural practices in their wake. Taiwan's multiculturalism, which as noted is deep and abundant, stems first and foremost from the nation's own native, aboriginal peoples. Fourteen aboriginal tribes are now recognized by the Taiwan government, each with their own languages and traditions (and several more are waiting in the wings for recognition). As noted, in alignment with the out of Taiwan thesis, it is believed by some anthropologists that Austronesian languages across the Indo-Pacific region may have originated in Taiwan, with all the multicultural identity that could suggest. To add to this, Taiwan's multicultural society has been initiated in the modern era, not only by way of Taiwanese traveling around the world and bringing home cultural traditions and customs from other lands (as examined above) but also by the large contingencies of foreigners who have made Taiwan their home and brought their own conventions, beliefs, and traditions with them—to be sure there are many Americans, Australians, Africans, Europeans, SE Asians, Chinese, and many other nationalities who make their home in Taiwan. All of this combines and coalesces with local Taiwan and Chinese culture into bounteous new ethnic pedigrees that have truly made Taiwan a welcoming cultural landscape with a variety of intriguing aspects supplied by people from all over the world. The combination of Asian and Western cultures, particularly (but this is not to take away from the other national additions in Taiwan), is a fresh, modern, and unique new view onto human existence.

With Japan's loss in World War II, Taiwan's status and identity as a "country" entered a new and challenging period. Control of Taiwan after World War II was never concretely settled, and various notes and treaties that dealt with the issue avoided deciding on who would actually be in control of the island. This changed when the KMT, led by Chiang Kai-shek, leader of the Republic of China, lost the Civil War to the communists in China and retreated to Taiwan by the tens of thousands. They took control of the island in a brutal and domineering way (they were encouraged and approved by the United States as the victor in the war, but to be sure the United States never decided absolutely who would govern the island; the issue was considered undecided, which is in part true to this day). The Japanese actually surrendered to Chiang Kai-shek, and so he assumed the commanding position and Taiwan was "returned to China" (Chiang has two names, not uncommon in Chinese culture, 蔣中正 and 蔣介石, Jiǎng Zhōng-zhèng and Jiǎng Jiè-shí). Chiang and the KMT announced the existence of the Republic of China on Taiwan and seized control of all governmental and regulatory functions in Taiwan, imposing martial law across the country. Chiang took control and was recognized worldwide as a brutal authoritarian who brooked absolutely no freedom or sovereignty in his subjects. He instituted the "White Terror" in Taiwan for the next 30 years, a time in which much good happened (the "White") and very much bad (the "Terror"). The good included economic growth (to become the Taiwan Miracle from the 1960s to 1980s), in some ways greater freedom (compared to the Japanese), important changes in law that gave farmers and small business owners greater ability to thrive, improved water and power supplies, reform of the banking and currency systems, improved public health facilities, much-improved infrastructure, and the expansion of the educational system, including many new institutions of higher education. I will critique this development below, but to be sure this led to significantly expanded literacy and learning in Taiwan, which would be at the foundation of the Taiwan Miracle. These were significant advances, and one reason that, in spite of his failings, a few people in Taiwan still see Chiang in a reasonably positive light (Fig. 2.5).

After Chiang died in 1976, his son Chiang Ching-kuo (蔣經國) assumed power and launched the "Ten Major Construction Projects," which built new ports, an international airport, cross-island highways, electrification of railways, and more (note that Chiang Ching-kuo, though not so brutal as his father, and in fact relatively popular to this day in Taiwan, was also recognized as an authoritarian dictator; Fig. 2.6).

The bad under the Chiangs included complete suppression of all free speech and thought and that intellectuals, artists, political leaders, and thousands of ordinary Taiwanese were jailed and killed by authorities and law enforcement. Much of this was done under the cover of the claim that a communist rebellion was imminent, with the government still seeing the communist movement as insurgence against the lawful Chinese government. In this respect, at this time, Taiwan/ROC still viewed China proper as its legal domain and technically sought to recover the entire country and even Mongolia. All of these ideas have now been tossed into the

Fig. 2.5 Chiang Kai-shek in military garb

Fig. 2.6 Chiang Ching-kuo

dustbin of history, though you might still find a few KMT loyalists who hope for this to happen (and in fact the current ROC Constitution still in effect counts China as its own territory).

The 228 Incident during this time was an event of major importance that has reverberated to the present day. This event erupted when law enforcement officials arrested a female selling cigarettes illegally and injured her, which engendered an uprising by Taiwanese citizens. The military and law enforcement cracked down on the rebellion forcefully, and it is now believed that as many as 28,000 Taiwanese citizens were killed. This dark period of Taiwan's history is honored with a holiday today, and many local monuments and museums honoring the killed are found in Taiwan. The government has stepped back and apologized for what happened. After Chiang Kai-shek's death, rule under his son was somewhat more relaxed, but a major incident in Kaohsiung in 1979 saw a pro-democracy demonstration crushed and many of its leaders jailed. Chen Shui-bian (陳水扁) and Annette Lu (呂秀蓮), later president and vice president, were involved. Chiang Ching-kuo in some respects moderated his rule after this, ultimately announcing the cessation of martial law in 1987 (the period of martial law in Taiwan, from 1949 to 1987, is recognized as the longest in history). This in turn led to the creation of the first alternative political party in the country (the DPP), the removal of government officials who had held their seats since the 1940s (the "iron rice bowl" of unchanging leadership and the free ride it gave those in power), and the free election of Taiwan's first president, Lee Teng-hui (李登輝), in 1996.

All of the above, and many other social demonstrations that took place during this time, represent what Hsin-Huang Michael Hsiao has called "changing state-society relations" in Taiwan, stemming from the "collective pressure generated by a variety of social movements that finally challenged the authoritarian state-dictated state-society power relations" (Hsiao, no page number). Acemoglu and Robinson have called this the "narrow corridor to liberty," in which "the state and society balance each other out" (xvi). A culture needs "an assertive, mobilized society able to hold its own against the state's power" (Acemoglu, Robinson, 200) in order to develop liberty and in turn economic development. in To be sure just this has occurred in Taiwan, and a myriad of social movements has arisen since the 1980s.

In 2000, the nation saw its first peaceful transfer of power between the KMT and DPP parties, and this has happened two more times since then.

Taiwan had arrived as a peaceful democracy and constitutional government guaranteeing freedom of speech and many other rights and civil liberties.

James Bohman (professor emeritus, philosophy, St. Louis University) summarizes the "ideal procedure" of democratic deliberation, including the following, which Taiwan adheres to assiduously:

1. Inclusion of everyone affected by the decision.
2. Substantive political equality includes opportunity to participate in deliberation.
3. Equality in methods of decision making and in determining the agenda.
4. Free and open exchange of information and reasons sufficient to acquire an understanding of both the issue in question and the opinions of others. (Welton, no page number)

Freedom House regularly ranks Taiwan as a "free" country, and the Human Freedom Index released by Canada's Fraser Institute and other international public policy think tanks ranked Taiwan as the 10th freest country in 2018. These developments are recognized as some of the most important international advances in the last 50 years.

With all of the above said about Taiwan's historical background and how the nation has reached its present state, I have written work for the *Taipei Times*, which looked at "history" in Taiwan and what it means for the peoples here, their identity, their uniqueness, and their own narrative. My aim was the creation of a coherent and constructive historical account for Taiwan, which seems in some ways to be lacking (but this is not to deny that Taiwan has exactly this, with a rich historical heritage and legacy conditioned by many different peoples and cultures). I have looked at the existence of a unique Taiwanese identity and its problems and challenges, not least because of the presence of strong Chinese cultural conditioning and historical connections. Additionally, the impact of foreign cultures and colonization, alongside Taiwanese traditions and ethnicity, as well as a number of other Asian influences, make the admixture of Taiwanese culture and identity yet more complex (identity will be examined in much more detail in a following chapter). I will not share my published work here, as it was published in my memoir.

Broadly, I continued my examination of Taiwan's historical narrative in another piece, basing my analysis on Francis Fukuyama's *The End of*

History and the Last Man, which posited that humanity had reached the "end" of its sociopolitical and historical development because of the widespread adoption of free, liberal political orders (and at the time of the publication of this book, the fall of the USSR). To be sure Taiwan traveled such a path in the 1980s and 1990s, leaving behind its tragic authoritarian past, embracing freedom and democracy, and in effect creating a new and positive historical direction for the nation. This fact has been widely celebrated by many observers worldwide. US Secretary of State Mike Pompeo told the 19th Micronesia Presidents' Summit in Palau in February 2019 that "Taiwan is...a democratic success story, a reliable partner and a force for good in the world" (*Taipei Times*, September 28, 2019). In a related turn, in President Ronald Reagan's "six assurances" to Taiwan in 1982, the United States stated that it would not formally recognize Chinese sovereignty over Taiwan. (US presidents since Reagan have generally been favorable to Taiwan, although George H.W. Bush, once ambassador to China, has been called that country's "old friend.")

Though less than openly critical of the People's Republic of China (PRC) in this work—I always endeavor to take a balanced and critically informed view—I do point to the significant disparities between China and Taiwan and a given negative in terms of politics and culture on the other side of the Taiwan Strait (i.e., the difference between authoritarianism and free democracy). In sum, I celebrate the strengths of Taiwan's free and independent republicanism, which recognizes each citizen as self-governing and sovereign. This work was published in the *Taipei Times* on March 9, 2018.

Good Things Happening in Taiwan

Published in 1992, Francis Fukuyama's *The End of History and the Last Man* had a significant impact on the political and social thinking at the time. Fukuyama's thesis was that humanity had reached the "end" of its sociopolitical development, due to the then widespread adoption of free, liberal political orders and the fall of the USSR.

Democracy had, seemingly, supplanted any alternative political structures, including monarchical, authoritarian, fascist/totalitarian, communist/socialist, theocratic, aristocratic, and absolutist (marginal theories like feminism, communitarianism, or libertarianism are given short shrift in the book).

Free, liberal political philosophy was the endpoint of a universal, developmental history in which humanity had for centuries searched for the ideal polity to govern and justify itself.

Such essential ideas about the value of liberal political orders and freedom are relevant to life in Taiwan.

Taiwan is far from the oldest free, liberal democratic order in the world—it is one of the newer—but the essential ideas have become ingrained in the Taiwanese mind.

With the "end of [political] history" and the existence of the "last [political] man," humans have found self-mastery and true sovereignty in their polities. In such a state, humans "are aware of their own true natures, and are able to fashion a political community that exists in conformity with those natures," Fukuyama said.

I sense that Taiwanese feel exactly this.

At heart, Fukuyama's thesis was that the "desire for recognition"—that is, recognition within one's society of one's humanity, basic human entitlements, dignity and worth, right to freedom, and equality in relations—has led to the adoption of free, liberal politics, and this "motor of history" would put an end to a "master/slave" mentality that had dominated political history for hundreds, if not thousands, of years.

Related to this was a given "violent battle" in which a person would be willing to risk their lives, proving "beyond any shadow of a doubt to themselves and to their fellows that they are free." They were thus truly independent human beings.

The idea was hinted at by major liberal thinkers in the past like Thomas Hobbes and John Locke, but was not established until Georg Wilhelm Friedrich Hegel introduced it.

For Hegel, "an individual could not become self-conscious … aware of himself as a separate human being without being recognized," Fukuyama said.

Taiwanese engaged in a contest like this from the late 1970s, when they launched a drive toward freedom and autonomy. Many Taiwanese indeed gave up their lives during this battle and many others their freedom—and this to say nothing of those who did the same during the long White Terror era.

Taiwanese have proven themselves worthy, and this has resulted in a free and independent polity, which grants each person recognition of their civic selves and self-command.

Related to this is the idea of human *thymos*, the ancient Greek term for "spiritedness," the willingness to risk one's life for better ends, and a given jealousy of one's own and others' dignity.

Thymos is the motivator for the search for, and ultimately the granting of, recognition in public life.

Here again we see a Taiwanese reality, and one senses that the people in this land, in a thymotic turn, grant each other recognition as decent human beings and are deferent to many different political beliefs. This might even be at the heart of the legendary genial, welcoming qualities of the Taiwanese.

A thymotic search, and the ultimate granting of decent recognition to one's fellows, is more than simply desire for goods. Liberal economic orders have long been closely associated with liberal political orders, and some have believed that it is the eager search for material gain that is behind humans' adoption of democratic, liberal politics.

Fukuyama dismisses this conception, writing that a purely economic analysis of political development would be "radically incomplete."

Although capitalism and liberal democracy are closely intertwined, the quest for more material goods was not what drove humans to develop their best political orders and to be sure such desirous, covetous aims do not account for the vigorous, even-handed conception of dignified recognition.

In a word, free government "exercises a positive pull of its own" and "recognition allows us to recover a totally non-materialist historical dialectic," Fukuyama said.

Some might argue that Taiwan is different from what is described here. The economy and material gain seem to have had a strong pull in Taiwan since its development from the 1950s on. Are Taiwanese simply economic men, acquisitive souls that want nothing more than "more"?

There might be some truth to this, as one would expect to see in a developing economy, but just as well, free political thought and action have had a strong impact and positive pull in life here.

Taiwanese young and old have taken to the streets in energetic fashion since the late 1970s—and using such methods have managed to pull down an authoritarian apparatus and replace it with a free democracy. That, to be sure, is a lot more than just the search for material gain.

Needless to say, such methods exist to the present, with the recent Sunflower Movement and many protests and demonstrations surrounding issues like labor, taxes, and international affairs.

Fukuyama's thesis has often been criticized.

Jacques Derrida wrote that violence and inequality are rife in the world and that these factors have often stemmed from the very political orders Fukuyama celebrates.

"Let us never neglect … sites of suffering: No degree of progress allows one to ignore that never before … have so many men, women and children been subjugated, starved or exterminated on the Earth," Derrida wrote.

Even Plato wrote: "Dictatorship naturally arises out of democracy, and the most aggravated form of tyranny and slavery out of the most extreme liberty."

These thoughts might be worrisome in their way, but the actuality in this land is very different. Modes of suffering, subjugation, starvation, or extermination are far from the reality in Taiwan and such pessimism seems inapplicable to life here.

Taiwan is a prosperous, generous, healthy, and dynamic country that seems to be enjoying the best fruits of its political choices.

Another challenge to the "end of history" thesis is the growth in the economic and political power of China—an essentially autocratic state, nearly a polar opposite of the democracy in Taiwan.

To be sure, our neighbor to the west offers a radically different political view—and the People's Republic of China has had its own successes that cannot be ignored.

Is socialism with Chinese characteristics a viable alternative to what we have examined here? Not a few people have said so, and this could represent a very different end than that posed by Fukuyama. Or it might be simply the existence of more than one alternative—and not an "end" at all.

This question might be a toss-up for the time being, although I suspect that a more likely outcome will be China adopting free, liberal politics in the future, following the global trend.

And so, in this light, has Taiwan reached the end of its own history and are its last people walking the ground of its free polity?

In the end, probably not—and Fukuyama would agree, writing that "we are not at that point now" and our culmination is "provisionally inconclusive."

I do not suspect that Taiwan will be backsliding into authoritarianism anytime soon, but the relationship with China is a very, very big historical development that awaits a conclusion.

This is the subject of another essay, but whatever happens, I feel that Taiwanese will be making good things happen, exercising and expanding their free commonwealth and liberty in ways that I can hardly imagine.

And get ready China, for, as George Washington said, "Liberty, when it begins to take root, is a plant of rapid growth."

To turn to more about Taiwan's politics and life, one of the important connections to democracy in Taiwan is the idea of independence in the nation. This is a very sensitive issue, and I have found that although there are many advocates of independence in Taiwan, for the most part it is not well understood in terms of the realities of international affairs, politics, and law. The following discussion of independence in Taiwan is adapted from my memoir, *Something Super: Living, Learning and Teaching in Taiwan*.

There is certainly a large group of independence advocates in Taiwan, and I have on the whole respected this group. But the fact is that they are often growlingly angry, seething with disdain for any nation or individual who does not concretely support their views. I sense that the independence movement in Taiwan has suffered due to these zealots, and quite a few people look at this group and their crusade with their own scorn.

At a high level, Taiwanese citizens have to face the fact that this country is *not independent*, whatever sorts of *status quo* (the existing state of affairs), *de jure* (practices that are legally recognized, irrespective of whether the practice actually exists) claims advocates want to make that the island is "de facto independent." De facto independence is the preferred claim of many kinda-sorta supporters of Taiwanese independence, as it assigns Taiwan a nominal independence in the present day (though de facto's definition of "existing or holding a specified position in fact but not necessarily by legal right" is anything but nominal). One such commentator is Jerome Keating, an American writer in Taipei. In his "No one can take Taiwan's freedom," published in the *Taipei Times* on February 23, 2019, he began the essay by stating "Begin with the fact that Taiwan is a de facto independent democratic nation" and from there repeated the phrase "de facto independence" or simply independence eight times. That is saying a lot about a country that is only viewed as actually independent by 15 other nations worldwide (and this includes Vatican City, which almost does not count as a "nation" or "state;" much more on this topic below). I have said that this is a half-measure, and this claim has no credibility in international relations circles. The United States in 1776 did not just tell Britain and the world, "We just are independent now. It's a status quo fact." A solid claim had to be made; a written document had to be issued. Though admittedly the DPP's 1999 "Resolution Regarding Taiwan's Future" claims that "Taiwan is a sovereign, independent country," this is by no means a declaration of independence, and even this text is watered down when it states that this position is "a historical fact and a reflection of the status quo" (I do not have a link to this document, but readers can review it on *Wikipedia*, "Resolution on Taiwan's Future"). None other than Taiwan president Tsai Ing-wen (蔡英文) said on January 16, 2020, after her re-election that "We don't have a need to declare ourselves an independent state. We are an independent country already and we call ourselves the Republic of China, Taiwan" (https://english.president.gov.tw/News/5962). As I have explained, this simply is not true, and my advice to Tsai is, "Oh yes you do have to declare yourselves independent, it is the only possible procedure in modern international affairs." Tsai went on that "Maintaining a 'status quo' remains our policy" which I have also rejected. Overall, I am quite surprised that a president exhibits such limited, faulty understanding of this important issue, and I do not think it bodes well for the future of Taiwan diplomacy.

To return to the DPP proclamation, I reject the idea of *status quo* independence, and that Taiwan's status is a "historical fact" falls short of a declaration of a here-and-now, present-day fact. As will be seen in the next documents I have published in Taiwan, in which I examine independence, the nations of South Sudan, Kosovo, East Timor, and Palau, to name only a few recent additions to the world's independent states, have debated and addressed this issue and achieved the real deal—true independence in world affairs. Taiwan's position certainly looks less sure. US senior director for East Asian Affairs at the National Security Council, Dennis Wilder, said in September 2007 that "Taiwan's statehood was an undecided issue, and as such it is not qualified to be a member of the UN" (*Taipei Times*, September 1, 2007). I will return to this issue in terms of the UN, below.[1]

Let me turn to Professor Jens Damm, associate fellow at the European Research Centre on Contemporary Taiwan (PhD, Freie Universität

[1] And in terms of this and the following, note that Taiwan has full membership in 38 intergovernmental organizations (IGO) and their subsidiary bodies, including the World Trade Organization, Asia-Pacific Economic Cooperation, Asian Development Bank, and Central American Bank for Economic Integration. It also enjoys observer or other statuses in 20 other IGOs and their subsidiary bodies, including the Inter-American Development Bank, European Bank for Reconstruction and Development, and committees of the Organisation for Economic Co-operation and Development (from Taiwan.gov.tw).

Berlin). Dr. Damm has worked at Chang Jung University, Tainan, Taiwan, and was an assistant professor at Free University Berlin. He has worked as a research associate at Freie Universität Berlin, Institute of East Asian Studies, and at the Otto Suhr Institute for Political Science. From September 2008 to September 2009, he was a visiting scholar at the Institute of Modern History, Academia Sinica, Taipei (Taiwan's most important research institution). He is also a board member of the European Association of Taiwan Studies. His research interests include new media and the Internet, the Taiwanese and Chinese diasporas and overseas Chinese communities, and gender studies. I conducted an email interview with Professor Damm in November 2019, and we later spoke. He kindly answered questions I posed.

"From a theoretical point of view, it may be that Taiwan is not really independent," said Professor Damm, seeming to support my view. "But more important. There is *realpolitik*. As long as the PRC insists on a one China policy, I do not see that there will be any change. At the same time, the term *de facto*, if used from a pragmatic point of view, is not too bad." Though I have objected to the term *de facto independence*, I would perhaps not disagree with this view, as *de facto* (and the other terminology I have looked at) do at least indicate *some sort of autonomy* (I refrain from saying "independence") for Taiwan in the current state of affairs. But again, I do not feel this is truly enough.

Damm goes on (in terms I will examine below) that Taiwan has "its own military, treaties with other nations, a passport…and Taiwan has embassies." All true, and important in international affairs—but still not enough, as I will examine below. Damm then says that the *status quo* may in essence be enough for now and that "the West (US) definitely prefers the status quo" and Taiwan should "just keep the status. Any outspoken claim to change the name, to raise the flag etc. can be counterproductive." Damm seems to be implying that my own recommendation that Taiwan has no choice but to "raise the flag," and actually announce its independence, will not be productive. Well this suggests much more, for to be sure were this to happen the situation would be dramatically changed, and the response from China, principally, would take on vital new importance. I will investigate the parameters of these possibilities below.

Damm continues that China itself may be attempting to change the status quo, but he does not explain this in detail. China has been criticized for military flights and naval exercises broaching Taiwan's borders, and many other military exercises that in essence threaten Taiwan, and of interfering in the 2020 Taiwan presidential election, all apparent changes to the *status quo*; more on this below. "We have to be realistic about what can be achieved," continues Damm. "Xi is not the most democratic leader, it is not a democratic society, elections are not free. It's really difficult. To predict the future is tricky." After considering the unification of the two Germanys in 1990, Damm concludes that "there can be changes also in cross-strait relations which we cannot predict. But if Taiwan does not challenge the *status quo* ([though] it is of course flexible), then it is for China very difficult to openly change relations with Taiwan." Looking at German unification, which can perhaps be seen in terms of the unification of Taiwan and China, Matilda Coleman, writing in *Up News Info* on November 8, 2019, commented that "on the thirtieth anniversary of the fall of the Berlin Wall on November 9, the question of what makes a German, who belongs and who does not, [may] be as restless as ever." She speaks of "the nerve problem of German identity," and one speaker in the story says "We were never given the power to tell our version of the story." Some Taiwanese might say the same of how China views reunification, and to be sure this is a "restless" issue, and there is something of a "nerve problem" across the Taiwan Strait, with Taiwanese people seeking to tell their own versions of their own stories in these lights (https://upnews-info.com/2019/11/08/germany-has-been-unified-for-30-years-your-identity-is-not-yet/).

In terms of all of the above, and in relation to the above discussion, it should be said that "In Taiwan's domestic politics, the People's Republic of China is not only a significant factor, but also a major player. The PRC central government in Beijing has a clear agenda on Taiwan: to use whatever means necessary to eradicate the 'Taiwan independence force'" (Jih-wen Lin, in Schubert, 15). In fact, the PRC's intrusion into Taiwan politics goes beyond even this claim and the actions noted above and takes the form of a "united front" assault on Taiwan. The united front is a comprehensive approach that takes place across cultural, economic, and political spectra, in pursuit of unification by way of a political and/or military revolutionary (communist) struggle. China's "objective is to annex Taiwan using a step-by-step unification strategy, or even military force, which Beijing has not renounced," wrote the *Taipei Times* on March 25, 2019. I am sure I do not need to remind readers that these issues are at the core of the festering conflict between the People's Republic of China and the ROC.

To continue, I do not dispute that some definitions would more or less indicate that Taiwan is independent, such as British scholar Anthony Smith's claim that a nation is "a named human population sharing a historic territory, common myths and historical memories, a mass, public culture, a common economy and common legal rights and duties for all members" (*Civilizing World Politics*, 57). Taiwan fits such a definition, but it is in effect an incomplete story, as Smith's definition could probably be applied to any number of groupings of peoples, and in any case, whether a nation is a functioning state with formal independence under international law is another question.

Some turn to the Montevideo Convention held in Uruguay in 1933, which defines a state as a nation with a permanent population, a defined territory, a functioning government, and the capacity to enter into relations with the other states (associated with this, some will refer to a nation having its own constitution and currency, issuing its own passports, and having armed services). The Convention also states, "The political existence of the state is independent of recognition by the other states" (see the Montevideo Convention at https://www.jus.uio.no/english/services/library/treaties/01/1-02/rights-duties-states.xml).

All of the above designations would apply to Taiwan, as a state of sorts. But they do not touch on independence proper, under international law. It is such international law conditions and/or conventions that are really the roadblock here—or am I wrong? After all, international law in the form of a variety of UN conventions and announcements (not least the Montevideo Convention mentioned above, the United Nations General Assembly Resolution 1514, the UN Charter, the International Covenant on Civil and Political Rights, and the International Covenant on Economic, Social, and Cultural Rights) maintains the right of nations to establish their sovereignty and international political status without the coercion or interference of other nations. The UN Charter itself states, "Membership in the United Nations is open to all ... peace-loving states which accept the obligations contained in the present Charter and, in the judgment of the Organization, are able and willing to carry out these obligations." Taiwan meets these requirements, and these endorsements seem to indicate something relatively close to the independent status of Taiwan (or autonomy, self-government, self-determination, a given sovereignty, etc.).

As a person who has lived and worked in this nation/state for many years, I can tell you these suppositions and conclusions all seem true. However, this does not change the fact: Taiwan has never declared its independence nor held such status, as such (not counting the brief foray the nation made in 1895). Only 15 nations around the world currently view the country in this light. This low number has long been a black mark on Taiwan's international affairs and indicates how the country is "not a country" to many observers. In recent years, Taiwan has lost a number of allies, who switched recognition to China, including seven in the last few years under the Tsai administration. The recent loss of the Solomon Islands and Kiribati caused an international stir and led to the United States fiercely striking out at the states that had cut diplomatic ties with Taiwan, culminating in the passage of the Taiwan Allies International Protection and Enhancement Initiative (TAIPEI) Act by the US Senate in October 2019. With this act, the United States will "punitively reduce engagement with countries whose actions 'undermine Taiwan'" (*Taipei Times*, October 30, 2019). I will not comment at length on this issue here (more below), but I find the US actions to be in flagrant violation of decent and respectful international behavior. All of this takes us back to my original claim: Taiwan is not independent by law. Even major allies like the United States, the EU, and Japan see the country in a half-light and go so far as to concede that Taiwan is a part of the singular People's Republic of China—that is, "One China."

Below is my "New approach to diplomatic bind," which examines the Kiribati and Solomon Islands issue (problems that have beleaguered Taiwan since the 1950s), and attempts to frame the argument in a broader context. This work was published in the *Taipei Times*, October 6, 2019.

New Approach to Diplomatic Bind

Taiwan's recent diplomatic quandaries, notably the severance of ties with the Solomon Islands and Kiribati, are serious problems that must be addressed—to the extent they can be addressed at all. To be sure, with fully six allies having withdrawn recognition of Taiwan in the last two years, the nation of Taiwan faces a near-emergency. Of course, this is a decades-old issue, and virtually every other country worldwide has done the same thing in the last 60 years. Thus, it is not really surprising, and it is a challenge that Taiwan must regularly face. Taiwan's remaining 15 allies find themselves in a ticklish position, "supporting" a country (the ROC) that few other nations do, one which has largely been cast on the dustbin of history. What, it is asked, can Taiwan do?

We should note here that what the six nations have done with Taiwan in the last few years is their perfect right and prerogative. Claims that they should be punished—and the United States is that forefront here—are brazen and in essence illegal (call it interfering in another state's internal affairs). What they have done is perfectly lawful, hard though it may be to face, and considered a good idea by many. Critics of these moves treat them as if they are negligible affairs, and such an attitude is disrespectful to nation-states worldwide. These nations are making serious decisions about the international diplomatic affairs, and they must be treated with dignity in so doing. This insistence on retribution is shameless and must be abrogated.

To be sure, Taiwan's situation looks dire. It seems likely that many other countries will do what other recent countries have done (and as well what the other 178 UN members have done). In the end Taiwan could be left with no diplomatic allies. Taiwan may find itself one day in this position and there may be no other option. This is an uncomfortable reality to face—but perhaps not without a solution, as to be examined below.

Taiwan as a nation has very little status in the world, and the Republic of China is doing no better. Yes, this seems odd in terms of the reality of the nation of Taiwan, a country with culture, history, peoples/ethnicities, languages, geography, world trade, laws, customs, norms, identity, and a functioning government (with all of its associated necessities of nationhood). The simple reality is that this country does function as just that in the international system, and few other countries would doubt this. Indeed, many other countries have taken the ultimate step and "recognized" Taiwan/ROC as just this in the world (the United States comes that close, as do many others). But this does not alter the reality of Taiwan's diminishing role and connection in world affairs. A country with no diplomatic allies, after all, can hardly be called a country at all. There are a handful of such countries in the world right now (the Republic of South Ossetia, the Turkish Republic of Northern Cyprus, and the Republic of Somaliland come to mind).

There have been observers in Taiwan who have said that allies do not matter much anyway, and in any case the cost of maintaining the few allies that Taiwan has left—most of them underdeveloped and impoverished—is not worth it. These people argue that losing diplomatic allies is tolerable, and in the same light it would not be the end of the world for Taiwan if its diplomatic allies dropped to zero, as long as it has the support of world powers such as the United States, the EU, and Japan. I don't think this is being fully explained, and the cold reality of this happening is not being squarely faced. While no doubt important, the above entities are only three powers, and if the other hundreds of UN member states still refuse to recognize Taiwan, then that is not significant progress.

What would it really mean if Taiwan were reduced to zero? Could it continue to survive at all? It seems that it would not be much like survival, but one wonders if Taiwan could launch a new model of diplomatic concurrence, becoming a one-off, stand-alone entity that, yes, does not even need the recognition of others—it could still function as an independent (very independent) state in the world (some would say this is essentially the nation's position now). Quite frankly, I rather like this idea, and the introduction of an innovative new paradigm of international diplomacy could be a bold move by Taiwan. This might evolve into something of the stateless world, populated by "world citizens" who have abandoned those often labored, synthetic attachments to home nations, an idea that has created endless conflict in the world, and in turn given rise to jingoistic and populist/nationalist risings. Such an idea might alter the very idea of the UN, and we may find ourselves modifying relations into a new UM, from the French Union Mondiale, Global Union.

There are states even now that hardly count as states as such, but they are recognized by hundreds of UN members: the State of Palestine and the Republic of Kosovo, for example. Thus, it can be true that a "stateless state" can be deeply involved in international affairs (which most would say is true of Taiwan even now). Jilted nationalism stains these populations as much as any other state/country, and that is an effect we hope can be moderated and one day eliminated.

With these problems in mind, one suggested move has been for the United States to reestablish formal diplomatic relations with Taiwan, proposed by former premier Yu Shyi-kun on September 14. This is an absurd idea, not least because it would violate US law. Yu said he "believes under Trump, Taiwan has its highest chance to see the US officially recognize it, as Trump is a non-traditionalist who is not afraid of changing the 'status quo' to serve US interests." Possibly true, and something that knucklehead Trump might indeed attempt to do. But this would be a one-off move by the president and would not represent any particular concordance at all. There is no chance such an action could take place, and only a handful of the most fervent Taiwan supporters in the US government could think of suggesting such a thing. The US Congress and Senate would never agree to it, and the very idea of severing ties with

China—which would have to happen in turn—is outrageous and no doubt impossible.

I hope the above description can be seen in a positive light in Taiwan. The situation may look dire on the surface, and for that reason alone a new approach may be called for. Taiwan may be faced with "going it alone" in the future, but maybe that is not the worst possible outcome. Let the UM begin today.

With the above consideration of Taiwan's diplomatic allies in mind, one view expressed by Ben Goren in the *Taipei Times* on August 18, 2019 ("Taiwan has other options than UN"), endorsed Taiwan aligning itself with the international non-aligned movement (NAM). The NAM, established in 1961, is a forum of 120 developing states that are not formally aligned with or against any major power bloc. After the United Nations, it is the largest grouping of states worldwide. NAM has espoused global cooperation and is in essence a Global South collective of developing nations seeking to strengthen their positions in the world. It has in essence been an anti-US group, and in fact the majority of its members are anything but non-aligned. I responded and criticized Goren's editorial on August 24, 2019.

NAM Is Not a Solution for Taiwan

The main point of Ben Goren's recent opinion piece, in terms of Taiwan's international situation, place, and role in world affairs is that, aside from membership in the UN, there is another option—that is, membership in the Non-Aligned Movement (NAM), but I do not see this favorably, although of course Taiwan does need outlets to solve its international problems, stemming from its expulsion from the UN in 1971 ("Taiwan has other options than UN," Aug. 18, page 6).

In fact, Taiwan/the Republic of China (ROC) does participate in a number of international organizations that give it a role and voice in world affairs.

Taiwan has a seat at the International Olympic Committee, the APEC, the Asian Development Bank, the Governmental Advisory Committee of the Internet Corporation for Assigned Names and Numbers, and the WTO. There is a long list of other organizations Taiwan is engaged in, not to mention Taiwan's 17 diplomatic allies, which also offer it a place at the table in international affairs.

In many ways, Goren's argument depends too heavily on the fact that Taiwan/ROC has been disallowed membership in the UN. No doubt this is problematic, but, as Goren notes, the UN is "not the only global body of significance." Enter the NAM.

The above of course is the central issue and an issue with no easy solutions. I have many times in this newspaper expressed my views on Taiwan's international situation, the looming presence of China and its refutation of Taiwan's international presence, and at the extreme end, the possibility of either armed conflict with China or Taiwan's independence.

My view has been at times less than positive in terms of Taiwan's situation and the possibility of its solution to these difficulties. At the same time, few would doubt my positive views on Taiwan's international status and ultimate ability to stake its claim to a newly found global status.

To repeat, Goren's view is that participation in the NAM could be Taiwan's best answer to the international and transnational problems that beset it.

The NAM is in fact the second-largest international organization after the UN—and it is surprising that its 120 members could actually claim to be unaligned with this or that power bloc and other international organizations. Most of these same countries are members of the UN, and in this and other respects, they have in fact aligned themselves in various ways with other nations and positions.

However, is the NAM really the best approach? Although this alliance has some admirable aims, it has been virtually non-visible in international news since its founding in 1961. It is in effect a movement of developing nations of "the Global South," and this is hardly Taiwan's status.

The NAM has been active in the Group of 77, but Taiwan's economy is the 7th largest in Asia; it is seen as an advanced economy by the IMF and a high-income economy by the World Bank and is ranked 15th in the world by the World Economic Forum. In these respects, and given Taiwan's membership in the WTO and more, it is a first-ranked world player and is generally seen as such by other nations.

It seems that India and Pakistan were virtual emblems of the NAM in much of its early period, and you cannot say much about that relationship. It seemed to reach a pinnacle of sorts with the Havana Declaration of 1979, when none other than then-Cuban president Fidel Castro announced that "the national independence, sovereignty, territorial integrity and security of non-aligned countries" would be maintained in their "struggle against imperialism, colonialism, neo-colonialism, racism, and all forms of foreign aggression, occupation, domination, interference or hegemony as well as against great power and bloc politics."

Not a bad statement, but since when should we put much significance in that which comes from Castro and Havana? Today, Venezuelan president Nicolas Maduro serves as the NAM chair, not a leader many others want to follow. Furthermore, are we supposed to consider Venezuela non-aligned?

Whether "non-alignment" in fact accords with human rights, peace, and equality worldwide could be subject to debate. Many NAM members hardly support and endorse such views in their normal politics.

This is not to say that some of its fundamental principles are not commendable. Yet again, there is not much actual action in terms of these ideas via the NAM. This is not to say that freedom, equality, and human rights are not supported around the world, but that the NAM's actual upkeep in these areas is for the most part little seen.

I am not convinced that "alignment" with members of the NAM would necessarily be better than Taiwan's current relations with the United States, the EU, Japan, and any number of other nations around the world (and here we might point to President Tsai Ing-wen's [蔡英文] New Southbound Policy and note that it too has strengthened ties with others).

Taiwan can do better than this. Currently, many people around the world see the nation as a viable member of the international community, a sovereign republic that upholds excellent civic values and virtues.

Taiwan has many economic relationships with countries worldwide, is a tourism hotspot, has excellent soft power and skills in cultural exchange, and has been a technology and medical leader. The situation is far from perfect, but the nation can hold its head high as it waits for changes to be made.

I have chastised various half-measures taken in terms of Taiwan and its nominal independence, in that they do nothing. Other such statements include "one country on each side" (former president Chen Shui-bian), "special state-to-state relations" (former president Lee Teng-hui), "one China, each with its own interpretation" (to be examined below), or the above-noted "de facto independence." I would say the same of the current Tsai Ing-wen administration, which prefers the *status quo* approach (which in sum accomplishes nothing) and has not taken positive steps toward independence or anything remotely like it. I think I should say that I would probably not want to be in Taiwan if independence were declared, as a move like this would be beset with danger, a war with China could be likely, and nobody wants this. Let us consider this possibility. Though China's military forces are obviously much larger, and Chinese military development has proceeded rapidly during the last 40 years (China's military budget was $228 billion compared to Taiwan's $10 billion in 2018, with active personnel of 2,300,000 [armedforces.eu]), the probability of such an attack is generally considered unlikely for the time being. It is felt that, principally, China does not have the amphibious capability to transport sufficient forces to Taiwan. I have said in another work that the Chinese air force and missile force could be adequate to do serious damage and that a paradrop into the capital could potentially seize control of the government, at least for a time (China's missile force, some 2000 strong, is considered a serious threat to the island and is widely denounced). Were there an invasion, the likelihood of widespread resistance by Taiwanese citizens seems likely, and this would present serious problems for China. Yet more important, the Taiwanese military is considered by some to be prepared for this possibility. *Foreign Policy* wrote on September 25, 2018, that in terms of the Taiwanese military, "Chinese commanders fear they may be forced into armed contest with an enemy that is better trained, better motivated, and better prepared for the rigors of warfare than troops the PLA could throw against them." The Taiwanese military was ranked 24th out of 136 countries in 2018, with China ranked 3rd, according to Global Firepower. Taiwanese Minister of National Defense Yen De-fa (嚴德發) said in February 2019 that "The nation's armed forces can hold the line against China's People's Liberation Army" and is "capable of holding off any first wave of attacks" (*Taipei Times*, February 26, 2019). "We will use counterattacks and early suppression of the enemy, as well as other actions," he continued. Also in the *Taipei Times* on February 26, 2019, Taiwan's DPP Premier Su Tseng-chang (蘇貞昌), no doubt going too far, said he would "fight to the end" with China, even if he "only had a broom." On September 12, 2019, Taiwan's Defense Policy Division Director Teng Keh-syong (鄧克雄) was quoted in the *Taipei Times*, saying, "The main military threat still comes from China, as its top leaders have not renounced the use of force to invade Taiwan, have spent a substantial portion of the national budget on increasing its military strength and moved to quickly modernize its armed forces. By trying to unilaterally alter the status quo across the Taiwan Strait, China poses the most serious challenge for Taiwan's national security."

Stephen Peter Rosen, in his *Winning the Next War*, wrote of the necessity in military planning of defining appropriate strategic measures of effectiveness (strategic goals) and the importance of current, relevant information obtained about potential enemy plans (intelligence). These approaches can be grounded on attention to resources and a valuation of the internal and external environments in which a state functions. This is a complete view and one which Taiwan needs to attend to. In a word, I think these areas sound like excellent pursuits for Taiwan. Not that I am hoping or planning for war, that is to be sure the last thing I would want. Rather, appropriate strategy, objectives, and aims can lead to innovation, modernization, and in the broadest sense the accomplishment of *peaceful resolution*. When two sides in a conflict find that they know quite a lot about the other and that their strategies and aims are in essence in accord, then they can find that conflict is simply not a good idea (this might be said of the USSR and the United States during the Cold War, a sort of deterrence; I will not call it Mutually Assured Destruction). Simply put, at the highest level, Taiwan needs a peace-oriented *strategy*, which it can link to Chinese aims and intentions.

Dr. Damm spoke on this topic, saying "Military threats, I regard them more as China's way to force Taiwan to restrain from declaring independence. Most Chinese academics, and also a lot of officials, wish to have better relations with Taiwan, but as soon as the Taiwanese counterparts talk about 'secession,' there is no way." Needless to say, this is true, and Chinese president Xi Jinping has made it abundantly clear that secession of Taiwan (independence) would result in a military response. This of course is the bad news, which I have considered above and will more below.

Damm goes on that Taiwan must keep its economic relations with China in view, and these relations will contribute to understanding and better relations with the giant next door. To be sure, cross-strait economic activity has grown substantially in the last 20 years, and investments have increased yet more recently. Taiwanese firms have relocated to China, and there they have collaborated on joint ventures. In fact, this has been an issue in Taiwan, and the current Tsai administration has made efforts to entice Taiwanese businesses in China to relocate back to Taiwan, with some success. Gordon Sun (孫明德), director of the Taiwan Institute of Economic Research's (TIER) Economic Forecasting Center, said on June 11, 2019, that "The ongoing trade dispute between Washington and Beijing will compel more Taiwanese firms operating in China to return to Taiwan to avoid the United States' punitive tariffs on goods made in China" (*Focus Taiwan*). The number of Taiwanese investors in China is now a substantial economic force, with upward of 420,000 Taiwanese workers and managers. In 2014, trade values between the two sides reached US$198.31 billion, with imports from Taiwan to the mainland up to US$152 billion. In 2015, 58 percent of Taiwanese working outside Taiwan worked in Mainland China (*Wikipedia*, "Cross-Strait Relations"). To what extent this has contributed to a peaceful cross-strait *entente* may be debatable, but many officials in China and Taiwan recognize its importance.

To return to military affairs, in the event of war, there is the possibility of a counter-campaign by the United States and other nations. Though this possibility is not entirely clear at this time, it is considered a strong likelihood. Though all of this may seem to weigh in Taiwan's favor, war against China would no doubt be devastating—for both Taiwan and China—and to be sure it is hoped that this will never happen. I have said that we can give China credit—outside of some missile tests and a few air force flights near Taiwan (to be sure, threatening in their way), the nation has never made any actionable threats and has not in any way come close to launching such an attack.

In terms of threat from China and the hopes for peace across the Taiwan Strait, the following is a revised version of a work published in the online *Taiwan News* on September 13, 2019.

Taiwan's Own Meiji Restoration: A Chance for Peaceful Resolutions to Potential Crises

This editorial is an examination of threats to Taiwan based on Jared Diamond's recent book *Upheaval*, which examines how nations cope with crises, internal and external threats, violence, and change. A focus in the work is how countries evince selective change to manage difficulties, which means knowing what needs changing and in turn constructing a "fence" surrounding such difficulties, so a country can differentiate between areas in which it genuinely needs to transform and develop and areas in which it is in good stead and does not need to change. Additionally, methods embedded in a country's identity and values are important, as are a nation's leaders, decision-making practices, institutions and policies, self-awareness, conceptions of reconciliation and compromise, responses to past problems, and group interaction and consensus.

I am considering Taiwan in these respects. As I mentioned in my previous editorial, Taiwan does not seem to be facing any true "upheaval" (or collapse, cataclysm, etc.) in the present day. This does not, however, ignore the fact that there are problems that Taiwan faces—and some of these are serious and threatening. I am not going to address environmental threats here, important though they might be (Taiwan has experienced environmental problems, but they have stopped short of reaching a crisis stage).

Diamond examines wars that have disrupted societies, as well as external threats and internal disruptions. Taiwan has never experienced a true war and there are no truly significant internal threats in Taiwan's society—political upheaval, insurgency, revolution, and the like. On the face of things, life seems ordered and benign here, but we all know the potential threat that hovers over life here. Things may look reasonable in Taiwan, but the threat that China poses looms large. We must recognize China as exactly this—an external threat that could give rise to violence and which as well poses an economic hazard to Taiwan. In a word, these appear to be the major upheavals that Taiwan could face, and we must examine and consider them carefully.

In these lights, Diamond examines Japan in the nineteenth century and the threat that the United States posed to the nation when Matthew Perry's naval force arrived in Tokyo Bay. This was both an economic and a military threat, and we can view China as a similar twofold menace. China is probably far from landing on the beaches of Taiwan any time soon, but the very idea is taken seriously in many circles, and as for the economic hazard, this seems to be double-edged sword, on which Taiwan could spear itself by way of losing China as an economic partner (whether by way of an aggressive move from China or not) or by overdepending on the China market, and in turn losing much via a brain drain of professionals and business expertise relocating to the Middle Kingdom, as well as a diminishment of commercial interaction with other nations.

Needless to say, the US action in Japan in the nineteenth century led to the Meiji (Bright Rule) Restoration era, in which Japan decreed many changes in the nation's life and culture. This modernized Japan and brought the ancient kingdom into the modern era, a move it was very happy with. Japan utilized many of the 12 "factors related to outcomes of national crises" that Diamond describes in his book, and these will be looked at in more detail below.

Exactly what threat China poses to Taiwan has been the subject of many analyses. Some analysts do not see the threat as paramount, and it may be that China has little desire for truly threatening behavior, least of all in terms of the military. No doubt possibly true, and whatever "expansionism" China may be accused of, the truth is it has not been a genuinely war-making nation in a long time. But that cannot distract from the fact that China's military has readied itself for an attack on Taiwan, and to be sure China's leadership has not discounted this possibility. The thousands of missiles targeting Taiwan right now certainly evince a significant military threat. And so, the reality is there, the potential for a true upheaval in society.

The actual possibility of war with China and what it might involve may be a bit too complex for this article, but let it be what it is: a threat, a danger in the most ominous sense. Many observers have noted a good chance that Taiwan could repel an initial invasion from China. This is to say nothing of the potential of other nations taking Taiwan's side and aiding the country; Diamond considers exactly such assistance as an important factor in how countries deal with crises. In the same manner, Taiwan can look to other nations as models for best behavior. Taiwan, as a somewhat Westernized Asian country, has done something just like this for many years. At the same time Diamond considers what must be maintained of a nation's prior identity, traditions, and history. This may be an area that has not been looked at in detail in terms of Taiwan, whose very modernization and Westernization seem to veer from this necessity.

Taiwan is no stranger to conflict. The nation was bombed by the United States in World War II, was home to many Japanese troops, and sent many troops to fight for Japan in the conflict. There was also a significant presence of prisoners of war in Taiwan during the 1940s. There were a number of wars between Spanish, Dutch, and French colonialists from the 1600s through the 1900s. The Dutch, Ming, and Qing dynasties engaged in serious conflict. The KMT and the CCP fought a number of engagements through the 1950s and early 1960s, and the Taiwan Straits crises of the 1990s (and even recently) have been serious military engagements. In spite of all of this, it can be said that Taiwan has not fought a war comprising a large territorial/ideological battle front. Yes, arguably, even now with China there is a "war"—but not quite that. Taiwan's role in the Chinese Civil War can be considered, but outside of the fact that Chiang Kai-shek retreated here when it was over, Taiwan's was not a heavy presence. In all of this we see conflict in Taiwan, but for the most part these have been battles and engagements, serious in ways, but short of actual war.

In any case, it appears that a foreboding reality is present and must be addressed. In these ways, China is something of a "negative model" as discussed by Diamond. Nevertheless, I ask myself if Taiwan could be in store for its own restoration and renewal, based on the threat from China. This could be a positive outcome, a sort of reconciliation that could introduce Taiwan into the twenty-first century in new ways. I am inclined to create a version of Taiwan's own "Meiji Restoration," and in order to maintain continuity I will also call it "美濟" (Měi jì), a term I like with its meaning of "beautiful" on the one hand and "relief/aid, crossing" on the other. (I was also thinking of using the word 吉 [ji; lucky].) With this in mind, my hope is that Taiwan can "cross" to something beautiful, lucky, and beneficial by way of its experience of this given "crisis." Taiwan's future Meiji Restoration will be the subject of another essay.

To continue, I will examine four or five of Diamond's factors related to outcomes of national crises in terms of the threats Taiwan faces and the potential for disturbance in this ostensibly well-ordered society, with its peaceful outlets for national discussion and consensus. In the main, I see positives in these lights, though there are some troubled areas.

In terms of leadership, Diamond asks whether nations require crises to "galvanize them into undertaking big changes," and I think he is principally thinking about leadership. To what extent leaders significantly impact world events, as opposed to the view that leaders in fact make little difference, is debated. The question becomes one of policy and procedure, how a country's political framework has the most impact, as opposed to "great men" or women. In this respect, and probably needless to say, Taiwan is in a good position, as a free democratic nation, with rule of law and consent behind all the decisions that are ultimately made. Nevertheless, if we take a hard look at Taiwan's actual leaders, they have been less than significant. I have said in the past that Taiwan's leaders have tended toward trivial statements that have tried to garner popularity rather than make a true difference in world affairs. Supporting a given "status quo" does not make great leaders, and bolder action is called for. In the long run, we seem to see a lot that is "okay" about leadership in Taiwan, but not a lot better than that. If we believe that leaders really do make a difference—and I think most would agree this is true—then we are going to need to raise the level that we see in Taiwan.

The above said, Taiwan's democracy does put it in good stead. The public's voice goes far in identifying problems that the nation faces and in turn in "building a fence" around them in order to appropriately identify them, while leaving intact that which is good about Taiwan's polity (and no doubt there is a great deal of that). Where this could lead may not be known at this time. Will the people of Taiwan stand up and demand better treatment and a stand-down from aggressive behavior from China? (In some sense, they are already doing this.) The main point is simply that the people of Taiwan must be able to stand up for themselves and solve their problems suitably. This would be a reconciliation, which is seen by Diamond as a necessary factor in dealing with problems.

As far as getting help from others to deal with the main problem that Taiwan faces, again it seems that the question is unsettled. The United States has certainly been a good partner in many ways, and the things that have been said and done about Taiwan by American leaders have been better and better in recent months. That does not answer the final question, however, of what could happen if there were aggression across the Taiwan Strait. Here too we have no definitive answers. Any war with China (no doubt the most extreme outcome) would not be welcomed by any country, including the United States. Less than a war, hesitance is still visible. Giving up China as a trading partner would not be welcome. No doubt many countries are in a bind over this, and they are feeling the heat as China turns up the heat. If a crisis arises, Taiwan may have to just hope for the best. Diamond writes that crisis is "a serious challenge that cannot be solved by existing methods of coping," but this seems errant. In sum, whatever crisis Taiwan faces—from colonialism to authoritarianism to the pressing demands of running a democracy—here, here!—it seems that the nation's politics, people, and identity are in a position to deal with them. Yes, there will be thorny stages and problems, and to be sure China has not made things any easier. But Taiwan has made it this far with a gorilla on its doorstep, and so it seems it can make it further.

Diamond stresses the importance of national identity and the core values of a nation. National identity and its associated myths, ideals, and language offer a "shared pride in admirable things that characterize one's nation and make it unique." In these respects, Taiwan has crafted an exceptional and enduring distinctiveness in the world. Identity and values don't fight wars in the obvious ways (important though they may be), but Taiwan is on solid ground here. I have commented many times on Taiwan's freedom and democracy and the value that these bring to the nation. As far as more local, aesthetic, and/or home-grown values, the country is also in good standing and has in many ways been a world leader. Taiwan can be proud of its culture, ethics, and standards (imperfect they may be, but nevertheless very solid and upstanding), and the world has noticed just this.

If there were a crisis with China, Taiwan would be faced with "honest national self-appraisal" and a "willingness to confront painful truths," as

Diamond puts it. Taiwan would seem to be in good shape here, and I don't think the nation has ever been particularly dishonest with itself in all the challenges it has faced. To be sure, Taiwan appears to have a few such painful truths on its plate right now, and the time is here to address and appraise them.

Associated with this is the idea of accepting responsibility for one's roles, accountability, and obligations during any difficult period. The people of Taiwan are the key here, and we must trust that they will take on this duty with true gusto. Such a stance would win the respect of other nations and could even positively impact China. The Middle Kingdom may not wish to be making trouble and meddling with a responsible, essentially blameless world citizen.

My hope from here is that Taiwan can emerge from these difficult times and embrace, endorse, and establish a better and greater future for itself and its neighbors, by way of a renewal and restoration of fundamental principles and values. We can evince all that can be best about life and living, people and politics, state and status. May a beautiful, peaceful, satisfying, positive, and in all senses practical and profitable passage be produced for all.

To continue on these lines, and perhaps with a better outcome in mind, I took up a subject in the *Taipei Times* that has been in the news recently, the possibility of a peace treaty between the ROC (Taiwan) and China (the People's Republic of China). This is a very sensitive, complex issue that takes in much about culture, world affairs, diplomacy, and military power. I note in this work that the fact that the two sides of the Taiwan Strait have to this day not settled their differences is essentially unparalleled in world affairs and that the possibility of a peace treaty, though improbable, should be considered. Most commentators have been speaking out against this idea, a point of view I consider negative and unconstructive (and indeed, this work drew fierce reprisals on the *Taipei Times* website message board). This piece was published in the *Taipei Times* on June 13, 2019.

A Chance at Peace Across the Strait

Whether Taiwan should sign a peace agreement with China to end the Chinese Civil War and bring cessation to hostilities between the Republic of China (ROC) and the People's Republic of China (PRC) has been an issue in the news of late. That the two sides of the Taiwan Strait have to this day not settled their differences is troubling and in large part unprecedented in international affairs. I am reminded of the US Civil War, which did come to terms, perplexed with difficulty though they were. To be sure the reunification of the Confederate States of America and the United States of America—a major accomplishment in US affairs—would be a sticking point in the debate in Taiwan, the citizens of which for the most part desire no such unification (though the point is arguable, and there are Taiwanese citizens who do desire a permanent union with China).

KMT Chairman Wu Den-yih (吳敦義) recently said that a KMT government in 2020 would be "within its rights" to sign a peace agreement. ("Wu Den-yih says KMT could sign peace treaty if it regains presidency next year" February 15, 2019). This is a simplistic, mechanical view that does not consider what this could mean for Taiwan, China, and the world and fails to examine what any advantages and/or difficulties a peace agreement would engender.

Of course, in all likelihood, the PRC would not sign any such agreement with the ROC, given the state of affairs and lack of recognition between both parties (and the KMT needs to see this truth before it could in any way move forward; just as much as the PRC, the ROC is not actually in any position to do much of anything in terms of a covenant, because of these facts). This lack of recognition of the international status of the ROC by the PRC, particularly, makes this whole enterprise seem unlikely. That may end the discussion outright—and could end my comments here as well.

Democratic Progressive Party (DPP) spokesman Johnny Lin (林琮盛) has said that "Wu's so-called cross-strait peace treaty cannot guarantee peace; Taiwan's sovereignty is the only foundation for building peace and stability" ("Wu Den-yih says KMT could sign peace treaty if it regains presidency next year" February 15, 2019). This need not necessarily be true and is in essence a limited view. One form of peace agreement or another could indeed be based on Taiwan/ROC's sovereignty, and were this allowed and agreed to, a breakthrough could be near (and yet again we must add, "If the PRC would agree" but this may not be an impossibility, though to what extent this would indicate "one country, two systems" is a factor).

Chang Kuo-tsai 張國財, another observer in this debate, has stated that such an agreement would be "pointless," citing tired military "principles" and just-as-tired historicity in terms of peace agreements made with the Nazis in the 1930s. These agreements were to be sure hollow and futile, but they have little relevance in today's world. The twenty-first century is definitely not a world of such brutal, violent dictatorships (yes, there are those who would argue that the PRC is very much such a state). "Would such a move bring peace? Or would it consign Taiwanese to servitude?" asks Chang, but this is going too far and looking at the idea in the most negative light ("Signing a peace deal with China is pointless," June 5, 2019).

Lo Cheng-chung (羅承宗) has said that "the frequent movement of goods and people [across the Taiwan Strait] has shown a state of peace already prevails across the Taiwan Strait" ("Cross-strait peace treaty unnecessary, academic says," February 20, 2019). It was also reported that more than 2.6 million Chinese tourists last year visited Taiwan, and there are more flights between China and Taiwan than between China and any other Asian nation. No doubt this could point to the validity and usefulness of further peaceful efforts. The Democratic Progressive Party, meanwhile, has said it would subject any peace agreement with China to a national referendum. This is a good idea, and I have a feeling that the Taiwanese people might just agree to it, in spite of the complexity.

The fact is that the PRC was never at war with Taiwan, and this might also lead in a positive direction, though that Taiwan, as the ROC, exists in fact and law, would make things difficult. It would be the ROC that signed any agreement, which China would probably object too. But this might be sidestepped, with China agreeing to work with "Taiwan," which it recognizes as an autonomous state in its way—but not the ROC. Seeing our way clear to understanding of what the ROC is in relation to what Taiwan is would be necessary—and just as complex.

"Instead of asking China to sign a piece of paper that guarantees nothing," Chang Kuo-tsai queries, "the KMT should ask China to renounce using armed force against Taiwan and all plans related to that purpose." His second statement is true enough, but this does not refute the efficacy and rationality of the first. A signed agreement in international law would be, first, a breakthrough for Taiwan and China in terms of their relationship and, second, a step toward world peace that both sides could be proud of. In all of this, with the hostility and lack of recognition that hangs like a cloud over this issue, it would be necessary for China to clear the air and see the soundness of ending war and hostility. By no means a definite possibility, but this opportunity should not be ignored (by either party).

Some of the commentators I have cited would say that the ROC no longer exists anyway, and only Taiwan is left over. Of course, the PRC was never at war with Taiwan, and thus if there is no ROC, there is no real possibility of any treaty, or much of anything else. We might be thus forced to ignore the whole enterprise and drift back into the (at times reassuring) status quo, economic peace that is in effect. That might be comforting in its static, immobile surety, but leaves a lot undone. "Peace" might become "petrified" and "evolution" might become "abeyance."

The idea that Taiwan should amass a yet stronger military to somehow contest China (no doubt an impossibility), and in turn create peace, is a contradiction. Nations do not aggregate military force in order to make peace, they do it to make war. The resulting militaries, staring eye to eye across a line in the sand, becomes a sort of Mutually Assured Destruction, which admittedly results in a sort of peaceful belligerence, but leaves the citizens of the countries as hostages, repressed collateral. That is not peace.

The *Taipei Times* itself stated in an article that it would be "ridiculous that the KMT would promote signing a peace agreement…it is a 'one country, two systems' agreement and 'peace' is 'united front' terminology ("Proposed KMT 'peace agreement' a misnomer," April 3, 2019). More negativity and all of this need not be true, if China can agree to a meeting. Though again improbable, it might not be an impossibility, and the two sides could work on something—if not an actual peace agreement, perhaps an announcement, which would show good will on both sides and an effort to promote peace. That few would argue with.

And indeed, such an agreement, or announcement, could wipe the slate clean on the Chinese Civil War, a dark period of world history. Out of that war emerged the PRC and the ROC, for many years neither especially credible nor responsible actors on the world stage. In this light, a peace treaty or accord (or declaration or proclamation) would shine a new peaceful light in world affairs. Great nations endeavor toward peace, and this has long been an important fact in our world. It is hoped that Taiwan and China, now great nations in their own rights, can move in this direction soon.

To return to my main subject, independence and sovereignty in Taiwan, perhaps one broad alternative could be that Taiwan, with the cooperation of China and the United Nations, could become some sort of non-state member of the UN (an actual voting but non-state member, similar to the recent admission of Palestine into the UN). This may not be an ideal solution, but it is a step away from a meaningless status quo as the position now stands, which yields little or no status for Taiwan. Were China to insist that as such a member, Taiwan would then be a given region of China, most Taiwanese people would not accept this. There would have to be more distance than that, though no doubt China would insist on some such formal relationship. (China calls it "one country, two systems," as in Hong Kong and Macau, and this idea has been universally rejected in Taiwan; Professor Damm too says it "cannot work.") These are complex issues that will require the best minds and the best collaboration to solve, but I suspect that one day, in some manner, the Taiwanese people will have to face them. I wish them luck. I will have more to say on this below.

With the above said I introduce an editorial I wrote for the *Taipei Times* that addressed these main issues. "Taiwan independence: It's in the air" was published on November 9, 2017.

Taiwanese Independence: It's in the Air

Michael Goldfarb asked "What Is a Nation in the 21st Century?" in the *New York Times* on October 27, and to be sure that is a question relevant to Taiwanese people. Whether we are talking solely about the here and now or the idea of nationality in an even larger, universal sense can be considered. To be sure, this question, whether local or global, exclusive or all-embracing, lingers in the Taiwanese mind.

Goldfarb considered the Kurdish, Catalonian, Scottish, and British sense of nationality in his article. To be sure all of these identities have been subject to fluctuating, changeful dynamics in recent times. He did not mention Taiwan, an oversight. In any case, the independence movements in the first three nations here, particularly, are pertinent for Taiwan. And for that matter we could look at Britain and the EU, as related to Taiwan and China, which will be considered below.

Goldfarb considers that there is a "new" sort of national identity in the twenty-first century, largely based on the end of the twentieth century when "The challenge to the existing idea of nationhood began with the end of Communism" and the crack-up of Yugoslavia. But Goldfarb does not explain this any further. And this opinion seems somewhat mistaken. When the USSR yielded 15 new countries and Yugoslavia 7, these countries became independent nations in ways that were not dramatically different from other claims to independence seen in the last hundreds of years. In other words, they announced their own independence, created the legal agendas, and then became sovereign states. Just like that, they were liberated and self-governing; there was not some other factor that intervened. The same thing is brewing nowadays with the nations we have looked at and, possibly, with Taiwan.

So where does Taiwan stand; what is its status? Is it "really" a nation or not? If you asked a Kurd, Catalonian, and even a Scot, they would say "Of course. We are a proud sovereign people, with a unique culture, history and identity, and a given independence in world affairs." No doubt any Taiwanese person would say the same. But the doubters would nevertheless intrude: Fine, but are you *really* independent in the world? And then things begin to cloud—and Kurds, Catalonians, Scots, and Taiwanese would be forced to say "Well…not in the customary sense in terms of actual international affairs and world law." East Timor, Palau, and the Czech Republic, on the other hand, can all say, "Yes, it's positively true. We *are* independent nations in the world," and indeed they are. In this respect a declaration of independence is the key to achieving this, and such a declaration is legally binding in every strong sense of the idea. Whether Catalonia, Kurdistan, and even Scotland go this far remains to be seen—exactly as it remains unresolved in Taiwan. (Britain is different in these respects, for obvious reasons. The nation has a genuine independence that cannot be doubted. Goldfarb considers United Kingdom's independence within the structure of the EU; as noted we will take this up below.)

This of course is not an easy question for Taiwan, for we all know the threat of war with China stands in the way. But to cut to the chase, it is this observer's view that a declaration of independence is exactly what Taiwan will need. This is the only route to freedom, to liberation. Claims that a sort of referendum in Taiwan, with the people voting on this issue, could yield the final result are not accurate. Such a referendum would not do the job—which has been seen in Catalonia, Kurdistan (where referendums have made no true difference), and even Scotland, which rejected the idea.

This writer is not an ardent Taiwan independence activist (he is in fact more of a unificationist). But it cannot be denied that the majority of people in Taiwan clearly appear to be leaning in this direction and hoping for this outcome. And there is only one way that Taiwan can actually achieve this goal—by way of the government, with Tsai Ing-wen at its head. Only a government announcement and the creation of a legal framework in terms of global law will actually achieve independence—exactly what the other nations we have discussed did in their time. To be sure Taiwan has never done anything like this. The ultimate responsibility for this miserable fiasco rests on Chiang Kai-shek and his failure to achieve independence after Taiwan was ejected from the United Nations—but let's not focus on Chiang. We must focus on Tsai Ing-wen and her own negligence in making any progress in this direction. Needless to say, Tsai adheres to *de facto* independence and a given status quo in relations—spineless approaches to cross-strait association that have done nothing to advance Taiwan's interests in global affairs, to say nothing of not achieving anything like true freedom and self-reliance for the Taiwanese people. Tsai's talk of a "new model" may be useful in its way, but in fact does not break any new ground. This will have to change—though admittedly an actual declaration of independence may still be a distant possibility.

In terms of new thinking, we would like to make a suggestion. Far-reaching and impractical though it may sound, it could be worth thinking about. This is the creation of something like a "borderless" world in which all of these considerations and conflicts will not even be required or addressed. This could include entities like the EU—and not a few people have suggested that such a unifying body is needed in Asia. An Asian Union would be a reasonably practical approach, and the hope would be that this would be an environment in which borders are removed (the EU has indeed something rather like this, with the Schengen Area). Something like a "world passport" would take the place of all the separate documents that are now required to travel and prove identity and nationality. This would have to take place to the extent possible, and most likely many or most countries in the world would not go along with the idea of dissolving their borders. A lot more negotiation would be needed before we could get anywhere near this idea. But it still seems positive in important ways. Call this writer a dreamer, with a desire for true "world citizenship."

These options could possibly solve a lot of problems and allow Taiwan entry into global affairs as an essentially independent nation (but the final question of actual independence may still not be answered). As far as borderlessness, this can be seen in terms of Catalonia, which hardly has much of any border separating it from Spain. Scotland has shown that it would not be against this idea and that it would more or less gladly ally itself with England in a happy union. Kurdistan seems to be a bit different, and the Kurdish people seem to have a stronger independent sense, in which they are somewhat more separate and truly autonomous, not a piece of Turkey or a slice of Iraq. Taiwan strikes me as somewhat similar to Catalonia in this regard. Catalonia is a potential country within a country, with which it has very close economic, political, cultural, and linguistic ties. Indeed, the vote *against* independence there has been fairly large, because this group simply feels that Catalonia *is* Spanish and that Spain in turn encompasses, girds, demarcates, and circumscribes Catalonia. The same goes for Taiwan. That is, Taiwan really *is* Chinese in significant respects, culturally, linguistically, and even economically (not so much politically, to be sure). Though many people would not agree (they would indeed strongly disagree), the fact that China ceded Taiwan to Japan in 1895 seems to indicate that Taiwan was once indeed part of China. No, not the People's Republic of China, but the PRC is in fact what "China" is today and thus can be essentially connected to the China that was in existence in the nineteenth century. People were alive and Chinese in the late nineteenth century and still alive and Chinese after 1949.

This closeness (call it that) across the Taiwan Strait could be helpful in various ways: with an EU-like conglomeration, the possibility of Taiwan unifying with China (with a good deal of independent power, it would be hoped), or, most broadly, in the borderless world we have suggested.

Goldfarb points out that some 500 years ago a Polish nobleman was asked about his national identity. He responded, "I am of the Polish nation, of the Lithuanian citizenship, of the Ruthenian people, and of Jewish origin." This is the sort of borderlessness we have referred to and is akin to a Samuel P. Huntington's "Clash of Civilizations" thesis—but we will dismiss his clash and focus on what could be positive. That is, Huntington said that a resident of Rome could define himself upward as Roman, Italian, Catholic, Christian, European, and Western. This accumulation could be seen as a very positive binding covenant in one's identity, opening new worlds of possibility and connection.

The time is now. Decisions need to be made. This is the twenty-first century, and though there might not be a truly new idea of nationhood, the old idea and many connected and related ideas can be seen as positives in our existence(s) and identification(s). Step up Taiwan, make your voice heard in the world today. A new and exciting selfhood, both associated and particular, awaits.

I wrote another piece on independence in the *Taipei Times*, which discussed the issue in terms of a debate about independence being held in Taiwan (as opposed to independence proper) and its value, utility, and/or significance to the nation on the world stage. Here I emphasized that a debate in a free country is necessary on a topic this important. China, the "gorilla in the room" as I say, to be sure objects to this possibility and has often said that it would respond forcefully to the "splittist" independence advocates who seek to change the nation of China by removing Taiwan from its orbit and control. China passed an "anti-secession" law aimed at Taiwan in 2005, which states that "non-peaceful and other necessary actions" can be taken in order to prevent Taiwan's secession from China and which as well aimed for reunification of Taiwan and China; this law has been the focus of heated denunciation in Taiwan and in many other countries worldwide (see the anti-secession law at http://www.china-embassy.org/eng/zt/999999999/t187406.htm). This issue traces back to the idea of "one China in the world" and the creation of the *Republic of China* on one side of the Taiwan Strait and the *People's Republic of China* on the other has disrupted this reality. The world at large has in the main agreed that there is only "one China"—the People's Republic of China (after all, only 15 countries currently recognize the sovereignty of the Republic of China). The *Taipei Times* reported on February 24, 2019, that former British governor of Hong Kong, Chris Patten, had said that although "Taiwan has impressed the international community with its successful transition to democracy...the vast majority of countries sensibly follow a 'one China' policy." This has left Taiwan (the Republic of China) in a tottering position on the world stage. This argument is ongoing, and although it does not appear to really be at the fore in Taiwan (on which I comment below), there is to be sure a fairly substantial group of citizens who do endorse and hope for an independent Taiwan. The newspaper in which the following work was published, the *Taipei Times*, is on the whole an independence-leaning publication, although it is careful not to go too far and state its beliefs concretely.

In the end, much of the world recognizes that China is an authoritarian country that, under current leader Xi Jinping, borders on dictatorship (his assumption of a role as the "permanent" president with the abolition of the five-year presidency in 2018 only adds to this). That such a nation could exercise control over a "free country" like Taiwan is frowned upon. But at the same time, China is respected for its own sovereignty ("freedom" is not quite the right word), and it is this sovereignty that is recognized by almost all nations around the world. In this respect, whether the ROC should in fact go by the name of "Taiwan" or the "Republic of Taiwan" has been debated, and although it is largely true that the nation is called by this name (i.e., "Taiwan") all around the world, the tenuous reality of the ROC (Taiwan's official name) remains. A referendum was held in Taiwan in 2018—and indeed such referendums are a true symbol of freedom for a voting public (Taiwan's referendum law was enacted in 2003)—that Taiwan should change the name of the nation's Olympic team from "Chinese Taipei" to "Taiwan;" this referendum was voted down. Note here the name "Chinese Taipei," which is used by Taiwan in almost all international institutions in which it has any role or input, is frowned upon by many in Taiwan and in other nations and is seen as coercion forced on the nation by China. Taiwan agreed to this designation after discussions with the International Olympic Committee in the early 1980s.

China has wielded a big stick during all of this, and recently Xi Jinping made a speech in which he stated that a military attack on Taiwan's free democracy, in order to take Taiwan in as a region of China, is a possibility that the PRC does not exclude. "We have firm will, full confidence, and sufficient capability to defeat any form of Taiwan independence secession plot. We will never allow any person, any organization, or any political party to split any part of the Chinese territory from China at any time or in any form," he said (*Foreign Policy*, September 25, 2018). With the above said, this piece, "Free discussion on independence," was published on February 15, 2019.

Free Discussion on Independence

Two opinion pieces in the *Taipei Times* on February 1 expressed the conception and potential reality of Taiwanese independence and the need for ensuing community discussion ("Time for serious discussion," "Justice is about more than just Chiang"). I wholeheartedly agree with such a prospect. The need for debate and discussion of the possibility of Taiwan's independence is long overdue, and it is hoped that this will take place soon. To be sure, such a disputation is hindered in the international world, and this complicates matters in Taiwan, but we hope that this actuality will not prevent dialogue on this issue (to say nothing of its eventuality).

It may sound prosaic, but this *political* idea should be disputed in a *free republic*. After all, Donald Trump is deliberating a border wall with Mexico in the United States; the Yellow Vest Movement in France has disputed economic justice in the old republic; activists in China have sought more freedom and democracy (such as they can); and Iran has pondered the validity of support for terrorism around the world (such as it will). These are bureaucratic issues that must take center stage in municipal affairs, and so they do all around the world. That a key issue like the potential of independence in Taiwan is not at the fore in civic proceedings is a true setback. Though understandable given China's resistance, this is a negative in terms of the Tsai Ing-wen (蔡英文) administration. In a word, it seems that the Tsai government has not taken this issue seriously enough, nor introduced the dialog needed in Taiwan culture and politics (the issue is both political and cultural, reaching across partisan lines and into realms of consciousness and awareness, what is thought, felt, and experienced among peoples). Though the government's reluctance is understandable—the potential conflict with China is something few truly want—the prospect of independence should not be completely ignored. After all South Sudan, Kosovo, East Timor, and Palau, to name only a few recent additions to the world's independent states, have debated and addressed this issue and achieved the real deal—actual independence in world affairs. These achievements have sometimes come by way of violent confrontation, but these peoples were not afraid to take such steps. I myself hesitate to suggest that conflict with China would be acceptable, but it cannot be disregarded forever. Look at what East Timor went through to accomplish its dream. Admittedly, this was done with the cooperation of the UN, and this could be a possibility with Taiwan as well.

I have myself discussed the conception of Taiwanese independence in the *Taipei Times*, and I was in sum in supportive of this vision ("Taiwan independence: It's in the air," November 8, 2017). It is not, however, that I am an avid supporter of Taiwan independence. Rather, I feel that such an issue must be acknowledged and responded to by the public of any country. Communities should have the right to examine such an issue, and although they might not be able to conclude matters absolutely, they must be able to speak their piece, to make their position clear. China, of course, is one nation that objects to this approach. China's view is not going to change anytime soon, and this will present problems for Taiwan. But most worrisomely, this means that *debate in a free country* is being obstructed by an authoritarian regime. This must surely concern other free countries in the world. Perhaps, we may hope that, simply because a debate is being conducted, a panic will not erupt in China. Even Chinese people may largely agree that this itself is not the real problem. From here they might indeed question their own government's position (forgive me if this sounds naïve).

I do not support the idea of Taiwan as a so-called *de facto* independent state. There is only one true independence in world affairs, and that is *actual independence* (read: South Sudan, Kosovo, East Timor, and Palau). Halfway measures such as *de facto* such-and-such will not do. In turn, I do not believe the continuance of *status quo* relations with China will result in anything favorable to Taiwan (*status quo* is, by definition, simply a repetition of what has been true before, which to be sure is far from advantageous to Taiwan; this is another negative with the Tsai administration). Other possibilities can be considered: Unification with China, or something like "one country, two systems"? It seems unlikely, but probably cannot be counted out. A union with China, possibly with a number of other Asian nations? A good idea, but it seems that Asians do not think this way. "One country on each side," "special state-to-state relations," "one China, each with its own interpretation"? Basically, these are more ill-founded half-measures, as those I have looked at. Then there was Ma Ying-jeou's (馬英九) "diplomatic truce" with China, not a half-bad idea and in a sense grounded in international law and doctrine. The problem was that it strayed outside a truce proper and became an opportunistic economic approach, with such buccaneering disagreeable to Taiwanese people. The final consideration is whether the Taiwanese public, by way of a referendum, national vote, possibly a presidential decision or simply by conveying the opinion in clear terms throughout the citizenry, actually choose independence. Then things could get sticky with China, but to repeat, this is exactly what the nations we have examined did in their own announcements, as have numerous other countries.

Needless to say, all of this sources back to China, and to be sure China would not accept debate of this issue in Taiwan calmly. The same could be said, with some frustration, of a number of other nations. Many countries talk the talk, but do not quite walk the walk, when it comes to the possibility of Taiwan's independence. The United States, Japan, and the EU have all balked somewhat when it comes to the actual probability of such an outcome. This is unfortunate, but again not unexpected given relations with China, the gorilla in the room.

My view is that this discussion should be started among communities in Taiwan, a cooperative, coordinated, reciprocal way that rebuffs and dismisses any authoritarian conceptions (no offense, China). Taiwanese people want—so I hope—an open, peace-minded, egalitarian, wholly free, and self-determining consideration of this issue (though it seems they are not enthusiastically supporting it at this time, with conflict looming so large). Possibly at this point, maybe Japan, the United States, and the EU will step in, reverse their reluctance, and insist that the Taiwanese people have the right and the prerogative to discourse this issue freely—maybe. And this is when we will have to hope that other free countries around the world will also aid Taiwan. And maybe, just maybe, China will not disagree and will perhaps allow such a symposium to continue freely (it won't kill you China). We hope for the best in all of this—and we hope that this political issue can be discussed in unrestricted terms and soon. Good luck Taiwan, in your considered, calculated view onto your own future, whatever that may be.

While I am on the discussion of Taiwanese politics, I have in the past been critical of the system here. The two major parties, the KMT or the more Taiwan-centric DPP, are vaguely similar to conservative Republicans and liberal Democrats in the United States (it is thus a two-party system, for the most part, though there are other parties in Taiwan). Not unlike the United States, these two parties vie fiercely and often unscrupulously for political power, and to be sure they are the talk of the country at almost all times. Everyone here is either "Blue" (KMT) or "Green" (DPP), and this is the cause of harsh disagreement all the time. But as I see it, the KMT and DPP are much less "political" than what you see in the United States, and in sum they seem to be doing less for the country.

In terms of political parties, when you think of a Republican or a Democrat in the United States, you think of the distinctly different political views of the two parties, conservative versus liberal, strains of libertarianism versus radicalism/progressivism, corporate issues, gun control, class and income, and different approaches to freedom, order, and equality. You do not see such specifics in Taiwan, and it seems that the two parties are less focused on modes of governance, administration, and diplomacy, and they function more as cultural and to some extent nationalist/ethnic icons (this is not to deny that governance and law-making do take place in Taiwan). The KMT and DPP are, it seems to me, less absorbed with serving the populace, proper, and instead spend their time vying with one another for attention and framing arguments in heated, dogmatic ways.

Professor Damm commented, saying "in most elections, the green and blue point of view is very important. However, in reality, no matter who governs the island has not really the power to change the relation to Beijing." This comment reflects back to my claim that the two parties are not handling diplomatic manners ideally. Damm goes on that "It would be much better if Taiwanese parties would stick to a *modus vivendi* with regard to the relation to China." Well, with *modus vivendi* meaning "an arrangement or agreement allowing conflicting parties to coexist peacefully," that sounds good to me—but Damm goes on that the two parties must "focus on different policies and modes of governance in Taiwan" (I assume he means "better" policies and modes of governance).

Unfortunately, he continues, "too often the parties split because their leaders cannot work together," and as I have said, this represents poor modes of authority and oversight.

In terms of these two major parties, the three presidents since the first transfer of power in 2000 have largely been miserable failures. The first, the DPP's Chen Shui-bian, was arrested after his second term, charged and found guilty of fraud and unethical practices, briefly jailed, and is now kept under house arrest due to failing health. The second, the KMT's Ma Ying-jeou, started reasonably well, but his decidedly pro-China policies and an attempt to force through economic policies in this direction led to a major uprising led by college students, which seized control of the legislature for a time and ultimately turned the nation against the KMT and Ma (this was the Sunflower Movement, an important event in Taiwan, and will be touched on again below). In the following mid-term elections, the KMT suffered devastating defeats and for the first time the DPP took control of the legislature and many new cities in Taiwan. Ma was in turn put on trial over a wire-tapping incident and inappropriate political influence. Finally, although the current president, the DPP's Tsai Ing-wen, has vaulted back to the top with her re-election in 2020, she went through a bad period in the months and year leading up to this, with her approval ratings sinking to lows and her party losing badly in the mid-term elections in 2018. Tsai's record, while not extremely bad, is seen as spotty, and the loss of seven diplomatic allies during her tenure is seen as a serious setback; for all her claims to be ultra-supportive of Taiwan sovereignty, the nation seems to have taken steps backward under her. Tsai is decidedly anti-China, and relations with the great neighbor across the strait have sunk to a new low, which is often frowned upon.

On the above, readers are aware that the Taiwan presidential election was held in January 2020, as I was finishing this book. The result was a DPP Tsai Ing-wen landslide victory, which did not surprise many in the country. Tsai received 57 percent of the vote, compared to her KMT opponent Han Kuo-yu's (韓國瑜) 39 percent and People First Party James Soong's (宋楚瑜) 4 percent. Han, the KMT mayor of Kaohsiung in southern Taiwan, was never seen as a very strong candidate, a populist speechifier (and not a very good one at that), something of a rube out of the countryside (草包, cǎobāo, country bumpkin, which actually means "straw bag," which is reminiscent of English "hayseed"), and a seemingly malinformed politician who was at worst a near-pro-China/pro-unification advocate (not a popular view in Taiwan these days). He was also seen as a narcissistic, overdrinking womanizer (Fig. 2.7). Han seemed to always be saying the wrong thing at the wrong time, and he bungled the presidential debate, when he was seen barking at journalist hosts and in sum making a fool of himself. When Han won the Kaohsiung mayorship in 2016, it was seen as an important development in Taiwan politics, as he dethroned a 20-year DPP rule in the city, and for a time he looked like a kingmaker. With his candidacy for the KMT presidency, many accused him of abandoning Kaohsiung and failing to keep his promises. The *Taipei Times* urged Han to resign and went on that his "checkered record in office has been punctuated with wild promises...but few concrete achievements" (July 30, 2019). The paper went on that Han's electoral strategy was "maximum polarization of national politics" and the radicalization of voters, "vilifying the DPP as reckless and destructive warmongers who, if allowed to remain in office for another four years, would catapult the nation toward catastrophe." Han's expatiation indicates all of this and more.

Fig. 2.7 ROC president Tsai Ing-wen

Kaohsiung at the time of Han's election had long viewed itself as a progressive, forward-looking populace that had embraced ostensibly "liberal" DPP views. The truth is that it was never this, and in the main it clung to an essentially mainstream view in Taiwan politics, that is, an arcane, ultra-conservative, and in essence mal-informed world view. Kaohsiung was always the artless little brother to the more sophisticated Taipei and never in any way displaced Taipei as a government and national forerunner. Taipei meanwhile, in its own "refinement" (the word is no doubt an overstatement), tended to shift from one political view to another, altering from KMT to DPP to Independent candidates in its selection of mayor. (This is reminiscent of what we see in the United States. Outside of the 12-year Republican rule from 1980 to 1992, the United States from 1960 to 2018 shifted back and forth between liberal/Democrat and conservative/Republican rule.)

So, Tsai is back, and to be sure in many ways this has been seen as a positive, as she is one of the few female leaders in Asia. I predicted she would win early on in the process. I could see as well as anyone that Han was a poor candidate, for the reasons outlined above. In the end, he was simply a bad choice by the KMT, though they did not have much better in the wings. The KMT is a failing party nowadays (in spite of its victories in the 2018 elections, which were a function of Tsai's falling popularity and a general slowdown in the DPP; this has largely been reversed; the party maintained its legislative majority in this election, and a glance at a map of Taiwan shows it is indeed largely "green" now). The KMT has little hope for much youthful change and development in the future (no young people in Taiwan want anything to do with the KMT). For all its one-time anti-China/PRC views ("gentlemen cannot stand together with thieves" Chiang Kai-shek once said of the ROC and PRC), the party is now seen as firmly pro-China and, worse, pro-unification (and again, these are anything but popular views in Taiwan today). In terms of youth, Tsai obviously had the majority of these voters supporting her all along, and without question the youth vote in Taiwan has taken on greater importance recently (after the election and the resignation of KMT Chairman Wu Den-yih, Sun Yat-sen School president Chang Ya-chung (張亞中) announced that he would run for the vacated KMT post and that he would transform the KMT into "a party that belongs to the young generation" [*Taipei Times*, January 15, 2020]). The editorial cartoon below, by *Taipei Times* cartoonist Taco Lin, pretty much says it all about the KMT nowadays (taipeitimes.com).

Han Kuo-yu met his comeuppance when Kaohsiung voters angrily recalled him from office on June 6. In the follow-on by-election for mayor on August 15, Chen Chi-mai of the Democratic Progressive Party walked into the post, with seventy percent voting in his favor, 25 percent voting for Li Mei-jhen of the KMT (who saw her reputation destroyed when it was found that she had plagiarized her master's degree thesis at National Sun Yat-sen University—the degree was later revoked), and four percent for the Taiwan People's Party non-starter, Wu Yi-jheng. Thus, Kaohsiung returned the DPP to power, and to be sure was basking in its glory again as the true progressive center of Taiwan. Han Kuo-yu has no doubt seen his own reputation and career permanently sullied, and nobody in Taiwan seems to mind. And so, this was the result in Taiwan, and although Tsai has suffered a fair amount of criticism herself, she clearly won this round. As always, I look to the future with a hint of hope (give Han some credit, he conceded the election gracefully), and while not strongly supportive of either party in Taiwan as I have explained, I tend to agree with the nation's populace on this decision. I have, however, offered my own take and a bit of criticism of Tsai, seen in the following a letter to the *Taipei Times* on May 24, 2009.

Feedback for Tsai

When Democratic Progressive Party (DPP) Chairperson Tsai Ing-wen (蔡英文) took power, I was impressed—she seemed smart and worldly. But I am less sure now, given some of her recent rhetoric.

I think one of Tsai's problems is that she is proving to be something of a one-trick pony, with her acerbic diatribes against the Chinese Nationalist Party (KMT), mantled in gushy, facile populism.

Recently she claimed that Taiwan needs "the power of the people from the grassroots upward to fuel a social revolution" ("DPP wraps up sit-in demonstration," May 19, page 1). Her recommendation borders on the absurd, for if there is one populace that is decidedly not likely to launch a revolution any time soon, it is the Taiwanese.

In a similarly hyperbolic vein, on May 2, Tsai said that the freedom to assemble is the people's "last line of defense." While appealing as hype, we see here a worrisome propensity for alarmist imagery, and in any case a more accurate view would be that the freedom to assemble is one line of defense among many that a democracy makes available to its citizens, any of which might come "first," "last," or "in media res."

Along with these sentiments, Tsai urges a one-size-fits-all referendum answer to Taiwan's political problems. Again her exhortation is counterproductive and unrealistic, for governments worldwide regularly make decisions without such substantial civic input or measures. This is not to deride the 23 million folks in Taiwan, but there are decisions on which their aggregate input will not be necessary, and the fact is that decision-making like this is essential to the very idea of constitutional democracy (I refer the reader to James Madison's Federalist No. 10).

In sum, Tsai's views sometimes sound at best like something espoused by an ancient Greek landowner gathering at the agora, or worse, like the heated speechifying of a member of the Students for a Democratic Society or the toe-the-line oratory of a Soviet apparatchik. What is needed are the creative, constructive recommendations of an insightful contemporary leader.

None of the above is meant to imply that Tsai's complaints might not be valid. It is only to suggest that she attend to them in more pragmatic ways.

The idea of grassroots support has been mentioned, and it seems that this is a golden opportunity for the DPP to—with the assent of the people—effect needed changes in Taiwan. But rather than vain hopes for a "revolution," what is needed are sensible, inventive, on-the-ground efforts that will aid the people in practical ways, inform them about political realities and changing conditions, and involve them in the betterment of their country. Everything would follow from there. Now that's power to the people.

Unbridled agitation and choleric broadsides will only lead to dead ends in Taiwan. My personal hope is that rather than such foment, the DPP and the other parties and civic groups in Taiwan will begin to create sounder, saner, more accommodating, judicious, and productive dialog.

The above may indicate something I have felt about both the DPP and the KMT in Taiwan, which is that I suggest they stop being so *anti-everything* and start being *pro-something*. The two parties' unscrupulous pursuit of power at any cost has been seriously detrimental to life and politics in Taiwan. Not for nothing have many observers looked on the political culture here and said "Ridiculous, shameless, trivial parties, prone more to hurling chairs at one another during governmental processes rather than seeking answers and appropriate solutions to questions the nation faces." (See https://www.newsweek.com/taiwan-parliament-fight-videos-legislative-yuan-brawl-watch-638352.)

As noted, KMT Chairman Wu Den-yih announced his resignation after the election, a common occurrence with electoral failures in Taiwan. The next day seven KMT Central Standing committee members resigned to take responsibility for the defeats, with member Johnny Chiang (江啟臣) saying "To regain the trust of the people, the KMT must undergo a complete transformation" (*Taipei Times*, January 15, 2020). The KMT formed a task force after the election to review the setbacks and propose changes and reforms. KMT politician Chiang Wan-an (蔣萬安) said that the KMT must thoroughly review its losses and that its problems "would not be solved in a short time." No doubt this is true for this plummeting party in Taiwan.

China entered the scene after the election, spouting hyperbole and propaganda. The unification of Taiwan and China was "inevitable," said Chinese Minister of Foreign Affairs Wang Yi (王毅), but there was much worse than this (Xinhua news agency, in the *Taipei Times*, January 15, 2020). Wang went on that anyone who opposed his views would "stink for 10,000 years," citing a Chinese idiom that means one will go down in infamy (this idiom is unknown to this author). Xinhua went on that Tsai's party "had used 'dirty tactics,' including fake news, repression and intimidation" and that "external dark forces," including the United States, had

had a hand in the election (the *Taipei Times*, January 15, 2020). None of this surprises anyone, with Chinese state media long known to be anything but unbiased and dispassionate.

Taipei Mayor Ko Wen-je (柯文哲) was once seen as a possible presidential candidate in 2020, but he declined (he may run in 2024). He said in the February 27 *Taipei Times* that the political environment in Taiwan was "uncertain" and" extreme." Much of this extremity stems from the "Transitional Justice Movement," which seeks to eliminate the traces of Taiwan's authoritarian past and has caused rancorous disagreements across party and cultural lines. One important issue in this movement is what to do with the Chiang Kai-shek Memorial Hall, a large hall which houses a huge, Lincoln-like statue of Chiang. One consideration is whether the statue itself should be demolished and the hall "repurposed" into an educational institution or arts hall. Another idea has been to convert the hall into a memorial of all presidents of Taiwan, not only Chiang. I would not disagree with these ideas. After all, I view Chiang as a ruthless, murderous dictator with misplaced, disordered political views (as do many and probably most Taiwanese). As the *Taipei Times* wrote on August 6, 2018, Chiang "arrested, sentenced, tortured and killed Taiwanese students and intellectuals without restraint, and suppressed the beginnings of Taiwanese democracy." So, a repurposing I think would be a good idea. In turn, the *Taipei Times* reported on January 14, 2019, that the military honor guard that to this day marches before the Chiang statue might be removed (Fig. 2.8). Although I can agree with this in terms of the guard's march in front of the statue, I objected to the idea of removing it completely, specifically the removal of the guard lowering the Taiwan flag from in front of the hall itself. I expressed this is a letter to the *Taipei Times* on December 20, 2018.

Keep the Honor Guard

I note in your newspaper an article in which the Transitional Justice Commission recommends discontinuing the honor guard that marches in and outside of the Chiang Kai-shek Memorial Hall every day ("Commission urges end to Chiang memorial guards," Dec. 18, page 1).

I would not endorse this, for one reason that the honor guard is such a popular attraction in Taipei. I have watched the men many times myself and they are enjoyable in their military professionalism.

Fig. 2.8 CKS Memorial Hall honor guard

Rather than end this practice, I would recommend changing the function of the honor guard from one that honors Chiang Kai-shek (蔣介石) to one that recognizes democracy and human rights in Taiwan.

Even in the evening, when the guard takes down the flag in front of the hall, that is close to honoring Taiwan the nation, as opposed to Chiang Kai-shek, the dictator.

Let the guard make a good statement about what is great about Taiwan and tourists will be as happy as ever to view this.

Looking further at Taiwanese politics, in spite of much of what I outline above, Kharis Templeman, in the *International Journal of Taiwan Studies*, writes that the "well-institutionalised party system [in Taiwan]...in comparison to most other Third Wave democracies is a model of competitiveness, consistency, and stability" (Templeman, no page number). Superior party system institutionalization "has ensured a credible alternative to incumbents in each election, enhanced the responsiveness of governments to citizen demands, and encouraged the greater provision of public goods and development of broad, programmatic policies." So that says something about the value of Taiwanese democracy, and I have myself said that governance and lawmaking do take place in Taiwan.

One important issue that is discussed in political circles in Taiwan, and which has often been broached and addressed by the government, is Taiwan's admission to the UN. Taiwan of course lost its seat in the UN to China in 1971, after a long battle conditioned by the Cold War and East-West confrontation. With UN Resolution 2758, the General Assembly resolved "to recognize the representatives of [the People's Republic of China] as the only legitimate representatives of China to the United Nations." Taiwan was then ejected from the UN. Then-president Chiang Kai-shek made a miserable mess of this situation by refusing to make any effort to reenter the UN or reach any agreement with China, and Taiwan has sought without success to repeal Resolution 2758, and to reenter the UN, since then. The current government has not made these efforts (these struggles in the past were made with the cooperation of several of Taiwan's remaining diplomatic allies, who still often speak out in favor of Taiwan's participation in UN affairs). Probably needless to say, most Taiwanese resent this treatment by the UN (in fact most Taiwanese journalists and citizens are disallowed from entering most UN buildings and events), and there have been many protests and demonstrations by Taiwanese people and supporters seeking recognition by the world body. "Taiwan deserves to have a role in the United Nations, just as any other country in the world," Taiwan's foreign minister, Joseph Wu, has said (*New York Times*, September 21, 2018).

After the 1971 declaration, Taiwan was often referred to as a "Province of China," which is still largely in effect around the world, but many people strongly disagree with this (indeed, this has been an ongoing problem for Taiwan, including China's recent move to force a number of international airlines and companies to alter their websites, changing the designation of "Taiwan" to "Taiwan, province of China"; the Middle Kingdom was reasonably successful with this). As noted, demonstrations have taken place in Taiwan, the United States, and other countries seeking to rectify the situation and "bring Taiwan to the international table," though usually as a non-state "observer." This has occurred with the World Health Organization, which accepted Taiwan as an observer from 2008 to 2015, under the name "Chinese-Taipei." This invitation was cancelled with the election of Tsai Ing-wen in 2016, due to China's essential hostility (Taiwan's participation in the International Civil Aviation Organization is also seen in these lights and has been an issue here). The United States has stepped up often in its efforts to support Taiwan, and indeed the US Congress and current president Donald Trump have been very friendly toward Taiwan, made significant positive remarks, and passed important legislation in these regards. In 2018, 13 US senators backed Taiwan's bid for observer status in the World Health Assembly, the decision-making body of the World Health Organization; there has been a call to invite President Tsai Ing-wen to travel to the United States to speak to the US Congress (in general not allowed by US law); President Trump made a phone call to President Tsai Ing-wen in 2016 to congratulate her on her election as president (to be sure an important event, given that she is the first female president in Taiwan and one of the few in Asia); Trump also signed into law the Asia Reassurance Initiative Act, which was beneficial in terms of arms sales to Taiwan; US warships have frequently sailed through the Taiwan Strait and into the South China Sea (which China claims almost completely as its own, much to the aversion of most other nations worldwide), which is done to solidify relations with Taiwan, in terms of freedom of navigation, and in order to maintain peace in the Indo-Pacific region; the Taiwan Travel Act, passed by the US Congress in 2018, has opened doors and "it should be the policy of the United States to allow officials at all levels of the United States Government, including Cabinet-level national security officials, general officers, and other executive branch officials, to travel to Taiwan to meet their Taiwanese counterparts" (*Focus Taiwan News Channel*, October 26, 2019), and as noted Republican and Democratic senators have sought to downgrade US relations with any government that shifts allegiance from Taiwan to China and to halt or modify US assistance. Just recently, on December 19, 2019, the *Taipei Times* reported that the US National Defense Authorization Act for fiscal year 2020 will require the Pentagon to create plans to boost Taiwan-US cybersecurity cooperation, support Taiwan's resolve to bolster its self-defense capabilities, and increase bilateral military exchanges (as well as to report Chinese interference in Taiwan's elections, an issue of significant concern in Taiwan, as noted above).[2] In terms of all of the above, other

[2] Note here that an "anti-infiltration" bill was introduced to the Taiwan legislature in 2019, which sought to "prevent infiltration and interference by external enemies; ensure national security and social stability; and maintain the nation's sovereignty, and its freedom, democracy and constitutional order" (from the *Taipei Times*, December 27, 2019). The bill targeted interference in Taiwan elections, but was criticized as harmful to any Taiwanese citizen, at home or abroad, who voices any disagreement with government policy, and in addition that no administering authority has been named. The bill was passed on December 31, 2019.

Fig. 2.9 US president Donald Trump

entities and nations have also supported Taiwan. In terms of the UN and Taiwan, I wrote the following piece, published in the *Taipei Times* on October 13, 2017 (Fig. 2.9).

Taiwan and the UN: A Castle in Air

Taiwan, the ROC, has made various efforts to re-join the UN, after it was expelled and China was admitted as the sole government of the Chinese people in 1971. At times Taiwan has made formal efforts, seeking the help of allies of the ROC and making official appeals to enter the world body. At other times, unofficial efforts have been made, with Taiwanese people demonstrating at the UN and in other locations. To date, all efforts have been unsuccessful, and Taiwan, the ROC, is not a member of the UN and can participate minimally in only a few of its organizations.

It is well known that Taiwan lost its seat in the United Nations to China in 1971, after a long fight that had been colored by the Cold War and East-West confrontation. At the time, with UN Resolution 2758, "The General Assembly decided to recognize the representatives of the Government of the People's Republic of China as the only legitimate representatives of China to the United Nations." (Taiwan has sought without success to repeal Resolution 2758.) Taiwan was then referred to as a "Province of China," a reality that is still largely in effect around the world.

But many people strong disagree with this. Demonstrations have taken place in Taiwan, the United States and other countries seeking to rectify the situation and "bring Taiwan to the international table."

The essential question that limits Taiwan's recognition by other nations, and its admission into the UN, is whether Taiwan, the ROC, is "really" a sovereign nation or not. Taiwan at this time has formal diplomatic relations with only 20 nations, including the Holy See in Italy, Taiwan's only European ally. For many people, the time is long overdue for Taiwan to be readmitted into the UN, and such a move would be a just solution that would allow fair representation of the 23 million citizens of Taiwan in world affairs. The Taiwan United Nations Alliance submitted a letter to UN Secretary-General Antonio Guterres recently that stated "Bringing Taiwan into the UN system will…help strengthen peace and stability in the entire Asia-Pacific region and make the UN better represented," aims that few would argue with.

Some in Taiwan argue that President Tsai Ing-wen is not doing enough to join the UN. Indeed, the nation has dropped most of its efforts to formally join the UN, with the support of ROC allies (this approach was seen most prominently in the era of President Chen Shui-bian, who sought such admission annually and said in an address in 2007, "we want to use the name of Taiwan to actively join the international community, join international organizations and join the United Nations, and help Taiwan establish a new identity and status on the world map").

Although allies such as Nauru have spoken on Taiwan's behalf, the country itself is making minimal concerted effort. There has been talk of a referendum to demonstrate the collective will of the people and announce Taiwan's sovereignty (this might include changes in the constitution), but no such referendum has taken place. Needless to say, China has opposed any such efforts. Their claim is that Taiwan is not a sovereign nation and that in fact Taiwan "belongs" to China, at the very least as a province of the mainland, with a small measure of independent power.

The DPP has stated that "In 1971, the People's Republic of China replaced the Republic of China as a member of the United Nations, thus making Taiwan an international orphan." Does Taiwan deserve such a fate? And most importantly, can and should Taiwan be allowed back into the UN as a participating nation? This is the essential question, and it is fraught with difficulty.

Though we stated that the Tsai government has not done much in support of this issue, in fact the nation is active at the UN General Assembly this year, employing "diverse channels [to] amplify its efforts" in this area. "The ROC government has requested that diplomatic allies speak up for Taiwan at the General Debate, and their permanent representatives to the UN will sign a joint letter…[dealing] with the issue of Taiwan's participation in the UN system in a fair manner consistent with the values of the UN Charter." The country has three aims in this effort: efforts should be made to let Taiwan take part in an appropriate manner in UN specialized agencies; Taiwanese people should be allowed to enter UN grounds when holding valid identification documents issued by their government; and the UN should include Taiwan in meetings, mechanisms, and activities aimed at achieving the UN Sustainable Development Goals. These are all worthwhile goals to achieve, and we wish the country luck in its work at the UN. (The above quotes and information are from a Taiwan government press release.)

To make matters worse, however, there are those who would say that Taiwan is not truly an independent, sovereign nation. Many points militate against this—the country has its own military, a permanent population, its own governing bodies and a president, its own legal territory, its own visa system and currency, and certainly its own longstanding culture and history. But the naysayers can argue that Taiwan has not in fact declared its own independence and that the vast majority of nations worldwide do not recognize the nation as such. This is a burden that weighs heavily on Taiwan and will likely prevent any possibility of joining the UN.

And so what is the answer? There is no easy reply to this question. Taiwan has a given "de jure" independence, but this has not proven to be enough on the larger international scene—and the country should not depend on such buzz words to solve its problems. A secondary solution could be something along the lines of "recognition" by the UN without actual membership (similar to Palestine, as a sort of "observer"). But would China allow this? Very possibly not—which may leave only one more possibility: the declaration of independence by Taiwan. This of course is another can of worms, which could at worst result in war with China. But it is the view of this observer that this may be the only solution to this problem. In recent years South Sudan, East Timor, Palau, and the Czech Republic have all done just this. There is no reason it should be impossible for Taiwan. Yes, war with China is a frightening possibility, but in fact many smaller countries have warred with larger nations and won their independence (East Timor against Indonesia is a good recent example, and indeed we would say that the United States was a much weaker country than the United Kingdom when they launched their independence drive).

This is not to say that we invite or look forward to such a war—but in fact it could be that if China were faced with the actual independence of Taiwan, it would have no choice to but to accept the reality and live with it in a negotiated settlement. Some have argued that China might not have the actual military ability to conquer Taiwan. Not only is Taiwan's military one of the more formidable in the world (ranked 13th by some observers), but many doubt that China has the actual naval amphibious capability to actually convey a large army to the island. No doubt China could do great damage with its missiles and air force, and a large paratroop drop could conceivably take over the government temporarily, but that might not actually win a war. In terms of negotiation, it might be possible to discuss with the China the possibility of an "alliance" or "reunification" that would give Taiwan independence, while simultaneously working with China in a cooperative way (this may be a "one country, two systems" formula, but best outcomes could possibly be agreed to by Taiwan). These are all big maybes, but Taiwan in all respects appears to be an independent nation with a proud, autonomous people. It has been noted that Taiwan, a vibrant democracy, has shown that a free voting public is possible in Asia—which China has often denied, claiming "socialism with Chinese characteristics" is the best answer. An East Asian Democracy Forum in New York last week discussed this, and experts pointed out that a Taiwan model and experience represent a genuine contribution to UN values, and thus the nation should be admitted.

Something needs to be done to get the ball rolling in the right direction. At the very least, the government of Taiwan should be taking stronger action and should—with the cooperation of China (and many another country around the world)—be trying to make UN membership and participation for Taiwan not just a remote possibility, but a reality. "The ROC government urges the UN to take seriously the fundamental right of the 23 million people of Taiwan to participate in the UN system." We hope this can come to pass.

Not least in terms of the above, I should mention the Taiwan Relations Act (TRA), passed in 1979 by the US Congress and signed into law by US president Jimmy Carter. The TRA was passed in the aftermath of the United States establishing diplomatic relations with the People's Republic of China, a development that met with severe condemnation and protests in Taiwan. The TRA has been the legal framework and basis of US defense, security, economic, and political engagements with Taiwan and is in some sense based on a sentiment of "strategic ambiguity" in terms of exactly how the United States views the relations of itself, China, and Taiwan. Professor David Bachman has discussed the importance of Taiwan to US policy. "The bedrock of American support is...Taiwan's democracy," he has said. And, "Democracy is the articulation of conflict of interest and shared interest" of the two parties (Taiwan Studies Program, University of Washington, https://jsis.washington.edu/taiwan/2019). On December 15, 2019, the *Taipei Times* reported that Japanese lawmaker Jikido Aeba had proposed that the Japanese government should commit to supporting Taiwan by legislating a law similar to the US TRA, in order to consolidate Japan's relationship with Taiwan. I voiced support for this view in a letter to the *Taipei Times*, published on December 18, 2019:

TRA-Like Law Welcome

In an article published on Sunday by the Taipei Times ("Academic urges TRA-like Japan law," page 1), Japanese lawmaker Jikido Aeba urged the Japanese government to "establish a Taiwan-Japan relations bill," based on the United States' Taiwan Relations Act (TRA).

To be sure, the TRA has long been an important US law. It has enabled constructive relations between the United States and Taiwan and not insignificantly created a stronger security partnership between the two countries.

Were Japan to do the same, it could very well open up a new methodology and construct in international law vis-à-vis Taiwan and the international community.

My point here is that the establishment of actual legalized relations between Japan and Taiwan could introduce a new internationalized legal order—outside of given "memoranda of understanding," agency agreements, bilateral accords, or generalized economic agreements (which this article concedes has been the primary focus of Japan-Taiwan relations for many years).

Rather than any halfway measure, such an act would be a legislated, fully lawful covenant, in which national and international collaboration and cooperation are emplaced in statute, precedent, and covenant. It would thus be more than a given "agreement," "compromise," or even concord and instead a fixed mandate of law itself.

It would be an international legal understanding—and virtually every country in the world today claims it "adheres to the rule of law," and this phrasing has become a code word and concrete element of just what it means to be a free international associate and accessory (not all nations can actually claim this, but they can always try).

To be sure, there would be complexities in such an act, in terms of military relations between Taiwan and Japan.

Aeba states that Japan should amend its constitution "to enable the Japan Self-Defense Forces to defend its Asian partners." This is probably unlikely, but given that the TRA addresses just these factors, there is probably no reason that Japan and Taiwan could not do something similar.

In a word, Japan legislating such an act would further legalize Taiwan as an international adjunct in the world, with what that means in terms of the rule of law and the role of free, constitutional nations in the world. This would all codify and further authorize the states of Japan and Taiwan (Republic of China) in international law and from there cement relations with their alliances and their association with other nations. China might not fully comply with these principles, but it could not deny that a new international legal order was in effect.

Who said it best? Austin O'Malley (American professor, 1858–1932) said that "Law is the rudder of the ship of state." The rudders of two ships of state, Japan and Taiwan, may be in the spotlight soon. Or US Supreme Court Justice Thurgood Marshall, who said "Do what you think is right, and let the law catch up." Let us let the law move ahead and strike new chords of agreement and kindred spirit with Taiwan and its partners around the world.

As I was writing this book, the *Taipei Times* reported on February 23, 2019, that "A delegation of members of the European Parliament…called for stronger political cooperation between [Taiwan] and the EU" and their statement that "What brings us together is the respect and sympathy for Taiwan and its people. We feel that we share the same values and principles," including freedom, democracy, the rule of law, respect for human rights, and an open society. In January 2017, Japan's representative office in Taiwan was changed from the Japan Interchange Association to the Japan-Taiwan Exchange Association, which "aimed at advancing already close Japan-Taiwan relations" (*Focus Taiwan News Channel*, January 3, 2017). China stated that it was "dissatisfied" with the change. The UN, meanwhile, has been somewhat less than inviting and, as noted, has prevented Taiwanese journalists and citizens from attending many activities and even visiting the UN headquarters.

While on the topic of politics and presidents, let me share a work I published in the *Taipei Times* on October 26, 2017. In this work, I scrutinize US president Donald Trump's positions and policies regarding Taiwan and China and the issues of autocracy versus free democratic orders.

Donald Trump, Taiwan, and China

This opinion piece will examine US president Donald Trump's positions and policies regarding Taiwan and China. No doubt the two sides of the Taiwan Strait have a contentious relationship, yet more so since President Tsai Ing-wen (蔡英文) was elected, and this association is fraught with difficulty—for all three nations being considered here.

No less than war has been seen as a possibility, which none of the three truly want, but which seems to be a real prospect. Even short of armed conflict, the everyday conceptions of economic, cultural, and political interaction are trying. Though distant from this challenging whirligig, Trump, as any US president, is a central actor. And so, what is Trump thinking, and how will he make his presence felt on this side of the world? Let us look at the options, with Trump and Taiwan scrutinized first.

In terms of Trump's policies on Taiwan, he met with approval at home and abroad with his telephone conversation with Tsai on December 2 last year. The call no doubt risked the ire of China, but it took place, with the Trump team remarking that the context was the firm economic, political, and security ties that exist between Taiwan and the United States —no doubt true, though rather than any genuine look at interaction and communication between the two leaders, this smacks of partisan speechifying (something that always mars Taiwan-US relations, weakening unaffected administrative and collective ties between the two nations).

Though friendly with Chinese president Xi Jinping (習近平), Trump has by no means openly discouraged Taiwan. At the highest level, he has approved a US$1.4 billion arms package to Taiwan—a very important expansion.

Meanwhile, the US Senate and House of Representatives have been most agreeable with Taiwan and introduced a number of bills that have been very favorable to the nation. Trump cannot ignore these legal legislative developments and will likely go along with all of them.

In spite of these positive qualities, Trump has not actually said much that openly supports Taiwan's sovereignty and/or self-possession (in fact, he has not said all that much about Taiwan at all).

Thus, in sum, Trump's approach to Taiwan has been obliging, but much less than openly supportive and encouraging.

"Donald Trump is no friend of Taiwan," the Foreign Policy Research Institute said recently, and this is worrisome.

In terms of China, it appears that Trump and Xi have forged a fairly cooperative relationship, particularly after Xi's visit to the United States at Trump's sumptuous resort in May (accommodations like this are bound to create reasonably good spirits).

"We have a great chemistry together. We like each other. I like him a lot. I think his wife is terrific," Trump told the *Wall Street Journal.*

It is just this affability that has led some observers to say that Trump is cozying up to an authoritarian dictator. This could be partially true, as Trump himself appears to have an autocratic streak in his personality—his forceful and antagonistic policies have shown this.

However, is he getting in bed with Xi? Probably not.

Though the two might have a genial connection and might even see eye to eye on certain restrictive, at times jingoistic, and even inequitable, policies, Trump is not likely to acquiescently hug up to China. The Middle Kingdom is too much a threat to US global dominance for that.

And, dictators have never really been that wild about one another—look at Adolf Hitler and Hideki Tojo in World War II, no particular friends they (and Hitler even dismissed Benito Mussolini as a second-rate totalitarian).

For Trump, China is a menace to US power, and his crazy-man US-first rhetoric will not allow Xi and his comrades to easily follow this route. The same is true for Xi, with his own nationalist bombast. I thus feel that although Xi and Trump look accommodating on the outside, neither is a best friend on the inside.

However, their sociability does need to be considered a bit further.

To be sure, not everyone in Taiwan is wild about the US and Chinese presidents being on a cliquey first-name basis. They would prefer the reverse, with Trump and Tsai meeting on the golf course or knocking back drinks at the Trump estate. Well, at least Trump and Tsai have made a substantive contact, as we have seen.

However, in the end, the reality is that Trump must put a lot more emphasis on the Chinese connection than he ever could on Taiwan, and good rapport with Xi is most assuredly a good thing for the United States, at least up to a point.

However, how far can it go? Could it be that the sociable, clubby Trump could end up consulting with China in advance of decisions about US arms sales to Taiwan, mediating with China, or formally recognizing Chinese dominion over Taiwan—thus violating former US president Ronald Reagan's "six assurances" to Taiwan?

I almost feel that Trump could be liable to make such theatrical moves, which would rock the political establishments of all three nations to the core—and that indeed sounds like Trump.

Though perhaps worrying, we suspect that the US Department of State would not stand for this. US Secretary of State Rex Tillerson—not unlike Trump a bit of a loose cannon (what would you expect from a Trump appointee?)—is not likely to upset the apple cart in such momentous ways, and many of his minions beneath him in the department would also not go along with such dramatic moves.

Speaking of which, I suspect the American Institute in Taiwan would be very much against such changes.

In the end, Trump's connection to Xi is probably for the most part a benefit—even a benefit to Taiwan. A pleasant relationship might lead to overall receptive negotiations, which could extend to Taiwan and its relationship with China.

Xi's oratory in last week's opening of the Chinese Communist Party's 19th National Congress might have sounded somewhat overbearing and negative toward Taiwan, but I bet that Trump—with his recent arms deal with Taiwan, his declaration that he was not inevitably bound by the "one China" policy, and his easygoing telephone conversation with Tsai—was in the back of his mind. Xi is no fool, and just as Trump, he seeks optimal relations with the other major superpower.

And so is Taiwan no more than a chit in terms of Trump's relationship with Beijing? No doubt this is a legitimate concern of Taiwanese, for Trump seems to play politics this way, moving pieces across the board game of political life in at best strategic, and at worst manipulative, ways.

This is a negative of Trump's personality and is a true concern for Taiwan—for it does indeed seem to downgrade Taiwan to a game piece.

China has said Trump is "playing with fire" in terms of his Taiwan strategy, but it seems that he has not really gone this far—and indeed he has not gone far enough. As noted, though agreeable, he has been much less than publicly heartening with Taiwan.

Considering the vital importance of the Taiwan-US relationship—not least in terms of a rising China in the world and the risk of conflict—this should be strengthened and improved.

Another issue that can be connected to the UN and other US and world affairs and Taiwan is a conception that has been floated recently by no less than the former vice president of Taiwan, Annette Lu. This is whether Taiwan should announce its neutrality in world affairs. Perhaps needless to say, this would make Taiwan the "Switzerland of the East," or a "light in the East," as I have described the country. Expanding on this, I wrote a letter to the *Taipei Times* on January 20, 2019, that discussed this conception:

Switzerland of the East

Jerome Keating writes how Taiwan could become the "Switzerland of the East" ("Becoming a Switzerland of the East," Jan. 15, page 8) and bases this claim pretty much entirely on Taiwan adopting a neutral stance in international affairs. I have myself endorsed this view in a piece in the *Taipei Times* ("Neutrality is Taiwan's best option," Oct. 6, 2008, page 8).

As I made clear in that piece, I very much agree that a neutral stance in Taiwan would be a peaceful and fruitful development, and I would still argue this is true. However, I think there may be even more similarities between Switzerland and Taiwan, and these should also be considered.

In terms of culture, education, and economy, considerations of similarities with Switzerland are in some ways already largely true, in the broadest sense. Taiwan has in some senses an economy based in part on agriculture, combined with small and larger industries, and a services/banking sector. These are all functioning well in Taiwan (similar to Switzerland, although we might add that Taiwan's electronics industry is far in the lead).

The GDPs of Switzerland and Taiwan are almost equal, according to the International Monetary Fund.

In some senses Taiwanese culture can be seen as almost equivalent to Swiss culture, with a notable history that even predates the establishment of Switzerland as a nation, and has had many prominent developments in music, visual arts, and literature. In some ways, the Taiwanese connection with Chinese culture—via opera, art, spiritual values, language, and cuisine—is even more ancient than Switzerland.

The population of Taiwan is much larger than Switzerland, and in this way, I think Taiwan is seen as an even more prominent nation.

In terms of education, Switzerland probably has the edge, but certainly we have seen some fairly impressive rankings of Taiwanese universities, and globalization is moving Taiwan higher and higher.

Probably more important is the similarity between Taiwan and Switzerland in terms of constitutional government, democracy, and freedom. Certainly, the nations are identical in these respects, and Taiwan, every bit as much as Switzerland (and perhaps even more so), has attracted international attention for its progress in these values and liberties.

The Swiss Federal Constitution declares the preservation of Switzerland's independence and the preservation of the welfare of the people as the highest objectives of Swiss policy. The same can be seen in Taiwan.

Switzerland's constitution broadly sets five policy objectives, which include the safeguarding of peace and coexistence of nations; the advancement of human rights, democracy, and the rule of law; the alleviation of poverty in the world and the protection of people during natural disasters or any other harm that is being done; and the conservation of the environment and precious natural resources.

In my mind, Taiwan is doing exactly the same in its national and foreign affairs, and this places this nation on a similar plane with a leading country such as Switzerland. Were Taiwan to add to this by announcing its neutrality with accompanying peaceful aims, then so much the better.

In sum, there is much indeed that is "Switzerlandesque" about Taiwan, and these values can be taken into a promising and rewarding future. To be sure, such as Switzerland in the West, Taiwan can be something great.

In terms of neutrality, to be sure I find this idea appealing and one that could be of great benefit to Taiwan's freedom, democracy, and peaceful relations in East Asia. J. Michael Cole, writing in the *Taiwan Sentinel* (July 12, 2013), condemned this idea, stating that "Beijing will not countenance the existence of equal governments, 'neutral' or otherwise." He goes on that "it would technically remove [Taiwan] as a crucial chokepoint in the first island chain and within the community of democracies in Asia," indicating a militaristic view. I have commented on neutrality in the *Taipei Times*, but once again will not publish this work here as it was published in my memoir.

Almost all that I have discussed thus far in terms of politics and culture in Taiwan is considered in another idea that is at the fore of discussion in this nation. This is the issue of a "consensus" that exists about Taiwan's status in regional and world affairs. A principal idea here is the conception of a "1992 consensus," supposedly coined after a November 1992 meeting in Hong Kong between the KMT and communist officials. At that time, a given "one China" framework was created, which stated that

"Both sides of the Taiwan Strait agree that there is only one China. However, the two sides of the Strait have different opinions as to the meaning of 'one China'" (http://www1.kmt.org.tw). I have always thought this claim can be relegated to the dustbin of history along with the other half measures I have mentioned (and to be sure many in Taiwan would agree with this). These steps have done little to benefit Taiwan and have muddied the waters of cross-strait relations and the status of Taiwan as a democratic nation for years.

I am reminded of American theorist John Rawls's conception of how consensus can be achieved. His idea was that a group of reasonable individuals, when deciding on social ideals ("justice" he would say), must be made ignorant of all social and economic data about themselves—including actualities of race, sex, religion, education, intelligence, talents or skills, and even the conception of the "good life" (the US Constitution's promise of "the pursuit of Happiness" aside)—and then asked to decide what principles should govern the political institutions under which they live. Such obliviousness is Rawls's famed "veil of ignorance"—the "necessary preconditions of communicative action" (Welton, no page number)—in which he argues that such an assembly would reject simplistic utilitarian principles, because no member of the group could know whether he or she belonged to a marginal group whose rights and interests might be neglected under institutions justified on these grounds. "Each person is to have an equal right to the most extensive basic liberty compatible with a similar liberty for others," said Rawls (Cohen, 692). I see these ideas as in accord with freedom and democracy in Taiwan, where the people seem to often be less focused on that which is specifically good for them and only them and more focused on the common good, seen from beneath the veil of ignorance—which all seems to be in accord with how rule "by the people" is linked to the quality and extent of public debate and how it can be protected from control by elites.

I have had much to say about consensuses in Taiwan. Below I include an initial look at the issue, written in a letter to the *Taipei Times* on October 24, 2016.

Taiwanese Imagining Taiwan

Jerome Keating ("Taiwan needs a new 'consensus'," Oct. 23, page 6) argues that Taiwan needs a "new consensus" to replace the (so-called, as the *Taipei Times* always puts it) "1992 consensus" and that this new consensus would be forged with Japan as an ally.

Nothing wrong with having Japan as an ally, no doubt that would be a beneficial confab.

And the "1992 consensus," whether so-called or actual, seems a bit of a fairy tale, with the idea of different interpretations of what exactly one nation comprises of, exhibiting an ignorance of what real nations are and encompass.

They are not subject to "interpretation," they just are—unified national entities with their own histories, identities, constitutions, ethics, morals, cultures, and the like. They are not two interpretations or readings at one and the same time.

In any case, rather than Keating's proposal, which sounds more like a straightforward administrative alliance than a new compromised understanding and elucidation, I would suggest that Taiwan come up with a new "consensus," but that that consensus stem from Taiwanese—no other nations, entities, or coalitions involved.

In other words, Taiwanese could forge their own national consensus, based on their own views of nationhood, character, the past and their own chronicle, public events, their particular heroes, political will, civic engagement, and identity.

The extent to which this identity identifies with China might be a sticking point and may require what I am suggesting to be rethought and retooled.

However, there might be nothing wrong with that and in the end maybe Taiwan and China will "unify" into a joint venture of sorts, with a combined view on all the qualities I have mentioned. It could be interesting and would indeed be a new consensus, possibly a very cooperative and advantageous one.

Whichever way Taiwanese go, in the end I hope that the consensus and the accord they fashion is indeed their own, their personal will and determination expressed onto an international (transnational, better) stage in an obliging, empathetic venture.

You go Taiwan, speak up and let us all know your own "interpretation" of the world in which you function.

The 1992 consensus claim has come under close scrutiny since its formation, and it is now said (by many, not all) that the term was invented by then-Mainland Affairs Council Chairman Su Chi (蘇起) in 2000, long after the original meeting. Today, China insists on one and only one China and that any consultations between Taiwan and China must proceed on lines of the 1992 consensus—which indicates that there is indeed only "one China." (That there are "different interpretations" of what this China may be seems absurd to me and wholly outside any reasonable and judicious conceptions of international affairs and negotiation.) Many in Taiwan, including the current Tsai government, reject this and will not endorse the 1992 consensus. Speaking at a 228 memorial in 2019, student activists stated "We believe that the phrase 'We are Taiwanese, not Chinese' encapsulates the greatest common factor shared among people of our generation. We do not, and will never, consider Taiwan a part of China" (*Taipei Times*, February 25, 2019). The *Taipei Times* has gone so far as to write "It is dumbfounding how a lie told a thousand times can almost become 'a truth' and be blown up to the point of having an effect on people's lives and threatening regional stability" and that "no consensus was ever reached between the two sides, period" (June 28, 2016). Connected to all of this, in terms of negotiation as endorsed by the communist PRC, is the above-mentioned "one country, two systems" framework, which is seen by the communists as the path forward for eventual unification with Taiwan. "China is still threatening to impose its 'one country, two systems' model for Taiwan," Tsai said in her National Day speech on October 10, 2019. "Their diplomatic offensives and military coercion pose a serious challenge to regional stability and peace. When freedom and democracy are challenged, and when the Republic of China's existence and development are threatened, we must stand up and defend ourselves" (Tsai, no page number). Rejection of this idea is "the most important Taiwan consensus," President Tsai Ing-wen said another time, and a true consensus "means people in Taiwan have to get together and form a consensus of their own and that they would then turn around and talk to the Chinese to form a cross-strait consensus so we can build a relationship on that consensus" (*Taipei Times*, January 7, 2012). That sounds good to me. As a true democrat from the United States, I believe in consensuses reached by the people of a nation, and I commented on what sorts of "consensuses" Taiwan might arrive at in the future in this work, published in the *Taipei Times* on October 19, 2018.

Building Consensuses Old and New

The "so-called 1992 consensus" (as it is often called) has a prominent place in Taiwan's politics, although it is subject to lots of doubt and debate. I take my place among the disbelievers and think that the "1992 consensus" is little more than a popular myth, in which the idea of "different interpretations" of what a country embraces is a mistake.

Rather than this fluctuating approach, we must view nations as singular entities, with their own histories, identities, constitutions, ethics, and philosophies and not subject to any other varying interpretations.

I conclude that what Taiwan really needs is a "new consensus" that encompasses its own view on nationhood, stemming from the Taiwanese. This consensual understanding, in other words, should be based on Taiwan's own views, its own disposition, its own past, and its own chronicle and identity.

At its heart, we are looking at what Taiwanese think of themselves—although the idea of a "consensus" suggests that others will be involved, which I think will be true in various ways.

One study of Taiwanese character by Liao Li-wei (廖立偉) in 2008 found that Taiwanese are utilitarian, superstitious, and practical and enjoy conflict.

Let us focus on the utilitarian and practical, although we will find that Taiwanese will get their share of conflict in the issues we are inspecting—and some would refer to the "1992 consensus" as little more than superstition.

The heart of the issue I am looking at is complicated by other factors and the extent to which this includes a sense of "Chinese-ness," or identification with China as a people and a nation, but let us focus on the central idea: what Taiwanese think of their own country, nation, and populace.

I have lived in Taiwan for many years and I should probably have an inkling of what exactly is involved here, but to aid me, I asked a Canadian-Taiwanese student at the National Taipei University of Business for his views.

To be sure, consulting young people has grown in importance in Taiwan, and they are no longer seen as the static receptacles they were once thought to be. (Think of the Sunflower Movement.)

The young person I spoke to expressed strong, coherent views on these subjects.

"My heart has always been with Taiwan, but I feel we are shifting. It does not matter that we do not have this [national] title if we come together and have passion, creativeness. I really think that the people of Taiwan are so strong, we can stand together," he told me.

This student summed up views onto what the concord we are considering might add up to.

Taiwanese certainly seem to be troubled by the questions that have arisen here. I suspect this is one reason that they have embraced a series of canards as I have examined, none of which go far in actually determining Taiwan's position and role in world affairs.

In a word, Taiwanese are not always sure what they constitute as a people and a nation. This is troubling.

To step back, evidence has shown that "Pacific populations originated in Taiwan around 5200 years ago," and migration from Taiwan "played a major role in the spread of people throughout the world" (Science Daily, Jan. 27, 2009).

In other words, the great Pacific migrations of yesteryear might have originated in Taiwan, and Taiwan might be the source of the great Austronesian exodus, with its many peoples and languages, to say nothing of the important technological and social developments that originated here.

These facts give Taiwan a view onto itself as an important global player, a cultural beacon, a technological hub (which is well enough known in the present day), and a source of human development.

These are all conditions and qualities to be proud of, and I sense that they could play a role in the development of a "new consensus" surrounding the nation's circumstances and status. The inclusion of Taiwan's aborigines in this debate would be essential in these respects.

I am not an expert in this area, but I know enough about Native American peoples—and the incredible embellishments that they have contributed to US life and culture—to know that this is a positive reality.

Like it or not, China has an important role to play in all we are discussing, and yes, this might be at the heart of any new consensus.

If we see Taiwan and China as strongly related and linked, this will open new doors, although it will also present problems to be dealt with.

However, this might not be a huge difficulty. In the end, maybe Taiwan and China will unite into a joint venture and combined world view at the center of a proposed new "Asian union." This could be thought-provoking and would indeed offer a new consensus, potentially an accommodating and profitable one.

"China is not a really a threat," the student I spoke to said. "People want to come together, we are human beings. We help each other with kindness, grace, pull together, we support each other as Asians. So we should stand strong, as Taiwan, we are a country. We can do well, if we respect each other, value each other, honor each other."

Once again, this student has pretty much said it all.

We might view this issue in terms of human, and particularly adolescent, development. That is, at this important transitional stage in life, people are deciding exactly who they are, what values they condone, their own mentality and psychology, and their roles among their associates. It seems that Taiwan is in a similar position.

This is possibly a result of Taiwan being something of an "adolescent" democracy in the world, and this raises another issue.

To be sure, Taiwan's arrival at its democratic position was the result of a thorough reassessment of its national character and potential place in the world from the 1970s to the 1990s. That this nation was able to make this transition indicates a deep well of maturity and good judgment that could be employed in terms of the issues we are discussing.

As an emergent and established democracy, Taiwan has stated its new position and rank in the world. This is a "consensus" that few other countries could disagree with or part from—yet again, China complicates matters.

However, there will come a time when China will have no choice but to recognize the reality that is Taiwanese democracy.

I have looked at various views in this essay. Combine these, and we might see our way to a new accord (if not a "consensus") of what Taiwan once was, has become, and what it might be.

We might see a concordance of what Taiwan is now, a new view that can be consensually embraced worldwide. With luck, China might see this as a positive, an effective recognition of just how great Taiwan is and how great China could be.

However, if Taiwanese reach these decisions, in the end I hope that the solidarity they fashion is their own, stemming from their resolve and purpose, expressed onto a transnational stage.

So I will say it again: Speak up, Taiwan, and let us all know your interpretation of who and what you are in the world today, your relationship to others, and your hope that you will be welcomed again into world affairs in the most accommodating and operational ways.

I have examined many difficulties and threats to Taiwan on the regional and international stages. Not least conflict with China, but there are a host of other possible concerns—threats to the environment, unsustainable societal practices, overpopulation, pressures on the government and potential upheaval, the nation's general international status and allies, and problems with urbanization and overdevelopment (Taiwan certainly has no problem with underdevelopment).

I scrutinized these issues in an editorial in the *Taipei Times*, basing my argument on the book *Collapse* by Jared Diamond. I ponder whether there is any collapse that can be foreseen in Taiwan's future. While an actual collapse seems unlikely, the threat presented by China could see something very close to this, and the other problems I have listed also present clear and present dangers, not least, in some respects, the dramatic "collapse" of diplomatic allies that recognize Taiwan, which has fallen from a peak of nearly all nations in the world in about 1950 to the current 15. Taiwan is now endeavoring to strengthen ties with its remaining diplomatic allies, even as some of them show signs of wavering and considering a switch in recognition from Taiwan to China. "We are doing our best to solidify ties with [our allies]," said Taiwan Minister of Foreign Affairs Joseph Wu (吳釗燮) (*Taipei Times*, March 5, 2019). This reality of Taiwan's allies switching diplomatic recognition to China due to economic enticements has brought accusations of "diplomatic poaching" and "checkbook diplomacy" directed at China by many countries (Taiwan has been accused of the same in the past and to be sure donates millions of dollars to its allies for economic, educational, medical, technological, and agricultural development; more on this below). It will require creative and bold action from Taiwanese politicians and citizens to address these and other complications in the future. Ultimately, "a society's responses [to threats] depend on its political, economic, and social institutions and on its cultural values," Jared Diamond says, and in this respect Taiwan seems to be in a strong position. Following is "Taiwan threatened by myriad risks," published June 6, 2018.

Taiwan Threatened by Myriad Risks

In his book, *Collapse*, Jared Diamond, a professor of geography at University of California, Los Angeles, examines a number of cultures, from ancient to modern, and how a number of these societies collapsed under various pressures, often ecological and environmental, and also because of political and economic tribulations.

Diamond's main focus is on ecology and the environment and how problems in these areas can result in social devastation. Most importantly, these difficulties stem from population growth and unsustainable agricultural practices, which often result in deforested areas, habitat destruction, soil problems, water management problems, excessive urbanization, and overhunting and overfishing. Ultimately, such practices result in food shortages, starvation, conflicts among groups, and even overthrows of governments. Climate change also comes into play here.

Another area is hostile neighbors—a reality that Taiwan can certainly understand. Trade relations, often with friendly neighbors, also come into play.

In the end, it is the local social and governmental response under different strains that will decide whether a society collapses.

"Institutions and values affect whether the society solves [or even tries to solve] its problems," Diamond writes.

With this introduction, I am compelled to ask: Is Taiwan in any danger of imminent collapse? This might seem overstated, for on the whole it seems unlikely that this modern republic, with its robust economy (a per capita GDP ranking of about 30th out of 187 countries, according to IMF statistics) and remarkable technological prowess, would be in much danger.

Yes, global environmental threats are a concern—not the least climate change and rising ocean levels—but such threats do not seem looming.

However, there is more at work here, as not only storied ancient cultures, such as the Easter Island or Mayan peoples, but also modern cultures are in danger of bringing their own demise through unwise and untenable systems and processes.

Diamond examines several modern cultures that might be under threat from both environmental and social or political factors, including societies in Africa, the Caribbean, China, and even the United States and Australia.

Being a modern nation, with extensive help and technology networks for all people, might not ensure complete protection from a potential collapse.

So again: What is Taiwan's situation?

Taiwan has faced a collapse-like situation in its politics and culture: It has lost four diplomatic allies in two years—Burkina Faso, Dominican Republic, Panama, and Sao Tome and Principe. Some people dismiss the developments as less than important, but this is not so.

What would be the case if Taiwan lost all of its diplomatic allies? Who would think that would be a favorable outcome? To be sure, it seems likely that something like this, or very near this, will one day eventuate in Taiwan, meaning the nation is faced with the "collapse" of its diplomatic unity and presence in the world.

Whether this would result in some greater social and political upheaval remains to be seen, but its severity cannot be dismissed. At worst, this could result in the overthrow of the government, with all of the disorder and turmoil it would bring. There is danger afoot, it seems.

The other major threat to Taiwan could be environmental changes and decline—at the very least this is a cause of concern for the nation. More than likely there might be internal problems resulting from environmental mismanagement, such as mishandling of farming, overdevelopment, and simply the exhaustion of the environment through pollution and waste.

Mishandled and exhaustive farming can result in soil degradation, deforestation, misuse of water resources, and clearing of natural habitats. It is said that agriculture in Taiwan has been so intense that soil degradation is an ongoing problem. A fair amount of farming is on slope lands, where soil erosion is a problem.

It could be said that Taiwan is an over-farmed nation, as it is necessary for the populace to feed itself to the extent possible, rather than having to import foodstuffs. Additionally, the forests, including ancient forests, have been cut back a fair degree.

Overdevelopment is certainly a problem in Taiwan, and although population growth has largely leveled off, the nation's population of almost 24 million people, with a population density of 669 per square kilometer, is somewhat extreme.

Feeding this large population is already a major challenge, and the pressures on farmlands are great. Whether this will outstrip local resources is a concern.

The major urban areas in Taiwan are gobbling up the landscape, and one can almost imagine Taiwan becoming a wholly urbanized island. A situation like this could result in a type of collapse, at least of the more pastoral, agrarian life. Very broadly, this might represent a spiritual collapse, a loss of a sylvan homeland.

Finally, the straightforward destruction of the environment by pollution and waste has been a problem for many years. The nation has somewhat of a bad reputation in this area. It is true that Taiwan has made some progress in this area, such as reduced plastic bag and utensil use, recycling, and the use of bags for household garbage.

However, other developments, such as offshore wind power generation, denuclearization, and solar power, have been delayed.

The threat of hostile neighbors is one of Diamond's foci, and an attack by China could result in true devastation and possibly a collapse of Taiwanese life and identity.

Whether China can, and will, do this remains an open question. It seems unlikely in the near term, but the overall possibility of this is far from remote, and the outcome, as far as warfare, would be horrific.

Connected to this is that an ostensibly friendly neighbor—China—can at the same time be hostile, especially if it suffers setbacks that turn the relationship around.

China is itself a threatened society, according to Diamond, and it is likely that it would withdraw economic and some measure of political support from Taiwan, which for better or worse is important here.

In all of these considerations, Diamond says that societies might fail due to four reasons: They fail to anticipate problems; they fail to perceive the problems as they take shape; they fail to try to resolve the problems; and they try to resolve the problems, but fail.

Such considerations should be looked at in Taiwan.

In terms of the environment and farming, the nation might be failing to anticipate the true problem—the same could be said of global warming.

Connected to this, the nation might be failing to try to resolve problems as they arise—look at how Taiwan has changed so little in terms of urbanization and ongoing environmental problems—and issues, such as nuclear power and the development of green energy, have not been fully addressed.

When Taiwan does try to tackle a problem, on the whole it is reasonably successful, as technologically advanced as it is.

In terms of trying, but failing, it is uncertain whether Taiwan-China relations do fall into this category. The government has for too long relied on tried-and-true "status quo" solutions to cross-strait difficulties, and this is in essence an ineffective non-solution.

The result is very few dexterous, pragmatic political ends are being sought and promoted. There have been steps to improve relations with China, and these might be commended, but the state of war and a general enmity that exists between Taiwan and China has far from reached any true solution at all.

This might be the time for Taiwan to revise certain core values and adopt new approaches, difficult though this might be.

Nations have done this in the past: Britain and France have ceded their colonial empires, Japan has retreated from militarism, the Soviet Union abandoned communism, and the United States in some senses has improved in areas that it once held close to its heart: racial and social discrimination of various stripes.

Taiwan should take a new stand vis-à-vis China—a more cooperative, symbiotic approach that might indeed treat all Chinese-speaking people as one big family.

The comments of Taipei Mayor Ko Wen-je (柯文哲) aside, that sounds agreeable and could prevent a devastating conflict.

The United States and Britain have generated such a feeling, and it has been for the better.

Taiwan needs to face some hard realities that appear to be on the horizon. Courageous leaders and a plucky public are called for.

Improvements in technology have drawn the world closer, and people are much more aware of all that surrounds us, as opposed to any society in the past.

There is an opportunity to learn from others and problems of the past, Diamond writes.

Ultimately, "a society's responses depend on its political, economic, and social institutions and on its cultural values," he says.

Taiwan might have an advantage in these respects, so let us see what it can do. The problems the nation faces will not be easy to resolve, but they are arising and must be dealt with, and now.

Taiwan politics, history, and culture: a grab bag conditioned by hundreds of years of interaction with many different polities and cultures, a great deal of conflict but also cooperation and comity, with countries all around the world. In terms of these issues, I was once involved in them in a significant way, during the job I had as an English consultant at the International Cooperation and Development Fund from 2000 to 2002 (this was briefly mentioned above). The ICDF is a non-government organization that works closely with the Taiwan Ministry of Foreign Affairs, organizing and managing the aid programs that Taiwan maintains in many of its allies. This was a job I loved very much, and I commented on my experience at this NGO in a letter to the *Taipei Times* on May 9, 2019.

ICDF Doing Great Work

After reading Juan Fernando Herrera Ramos' interview with International Cooperation and Development Fund (ICDF) Deputy Secretary-General Lee Pai-po (李?浡) ("The important role Taiwan ICDF plays in Taiwan's diplomacy," May 7, page 13), I would like to share my own experience with this organization.

I worked as the ICDF's English consultant for almost two years from 2000 to 2002. During this time, I worked on dozens of reports and articles that appeared in the ICDF's quarterly publication: "International Cooperation and Development," on its website (which for a time I redesigned). I edited many reports submitted by ICDF personnel from projects all around the world and worked closely with a number of foreign and Taiwanese professionals and academics who were also involved.

I even edited the work of former secretary-general Tien Hung-mao (田弘茂) and then-acting secretary-general Yang Tzu-pao (楊子葆).

It was a truly satisfying and rewarding experience working at this level on such important projects.

Needless to say, Taiwan's international aid programs did not begin with the ICDF.

The nation had been distributing technical assistance and aid since it first dispatched agricultural specialists to Africa in the early 1960s, but the ICDF has now taken up this torch in impressive and highly beneficial new ways and is a modern organization that is at the very forefront of international development—without question a major contribution in global affairs.

I could not agree more with this interview about the importance of the ICDF's generous work and the way the organization is involved in vital development projects in areas of agricultural development, public health, human resources, education, and business and technology.

To gain an understanding of the range of work I was involved in, I worked on papers and accounts about a bamboo housing project in El Salvador, a tourism development project in Belize, a fishery workshop in the Indo-Pacific region, a Panama fishers' loan project, cooperative flower production and marketing in Paraguay, and aquaculture development in Saudi Arabia.

It was all an amazing ride, and I felt honored to be so closely associated with these important global development projects. It gave me special satisfaction, as I had obtained a Bachelor of Arts in International Relations from San Francisco State University and I felt this was a true "international" position.

To this day I miss my station there.

One of my key responsibilities at the ICDF was writing an introductory editorial to the quarterly publication. Here I had the honor of writing a memorial after the 9/11 attacks, in which I asked for peace to prevail and that the ICDF and "all good and hopeful people" pledged "to forever remain involved in mankind, cultivating the best, most constructive, most life-affirming results" in their work.

In another I wrote of the dawning of a new age of possibility for the ICDF and that the organization was "staying the course" in its efforts "to create prosperity and social stability" in nations worldwide.

A high point of my experience could have been at an anniversary celebration—the ICDF was only five years old at that time—when I (almost) met then-president Chen Shui-bian (陳水扁), who had come to the office in Taipei's Tianmu District (天母).

In one work I edited in the quarterly publication, the story Hometown (故鄉) by Chinese author Lu Xun (魯迅) offered some valuable food for thought as we move forward on this cooperative path:

There is nothing concrete about the existence of hope. It is similar to a road. Actually, there was no road before a number of people have walked the path to create it.

With such aims in mind, I look forward to all the cooperative development work that the ICDF can do in the future.

In terms of the above, some might argue that this sort of work was a type of "checkbook diplomacy" exercised by Taiwan, and to be sure a great deal of development aid has flowed from the likes of the ICDF. Checkbook diplomacy was a charge long lodged against Taiwan/ROC, and there was probably some truth to this, as it was a method that ensured many states would continue to recognize the nation (in fact there was a letter in the *Taipei Times* on January 1, 2020, in which Geoff Merrill recommended that Taiwan should restart its checkbook diplomacy efforts in order sustain the count of its official allies; no doubt a bad idea that was not taken seriously by anyone). These days, it is more often China that is accused of this (and this accusation was lodged in the Kiribati/Solomon Islands affair, examined above), and the focus of Taiwan's diplomatic work is now "shifting from the one-way provision of foreign aid to two-way dialogue" (Taiwan.gov.tw).

On Taiwan diplomacy, I had another idea that I expressed in the *Taipei Times* on January 22, 2020. In this work I consider Taiwan's gubernatorial and statutory affairs, as well as its statecraft, and propose a schema that I believe could enhance these undertakings. At a fundamental level, I attempt with this idea to promote the ideal of personal righteousness and esteem in people who have acted decently, equitably, ethically, and most of all beneficially in Taiwan and world affairs. I make a proposal for a new effort by Taiwan to interact with the best "world citizens" and from there to reach nations worldwide with a positive and I hope valuable effort, rewarding these people and nations. I base my idea on Israel's award to the "righteous among the nations," which readers no doubt know includes an astonishing range of the most courageous and ethical people in history. In this piece, I suggest that Taiwan could do something similar and "pace its way" toward a brighter future.

New Award Needed to Honor Allies

I have an idea that might add something positive to Taiwan's diplomatic, governmental, and legalistic affairs and at a fundamental level promote the ideal of personal righteousness and prestige in people who have acted justly, conscientiously, and, most of all, constructively in world affairs.

More on the world at large below, but to begin, I am thinking of those who view Taiwan itself as an honored and esteemed nation among the world's peoples and who have taken steps to recognize and endorse this reality and introduce it to people everywhere.

I take this idea from the nation of Israel, which honors those who have protected Jews (primarily during the Holocaust) with the reverent praise of "Righteous Among the Nations"—recognition that has been granted to no less than 26,000 people to date. Among these heroes are the likes of Oskar Schindler, Raoul Wallenberg, and Saint Elizabeth Hesselblad of Sweden. Truly a righteous group.

That which is "righteous" is reverent praise, recognition of virtuous and distinguished behavior at the highest level, and, most importantly, awareness and acceptance of deep faith, support, and simply help for those in need. (My idea stems from the *Observer* article "A very quiet hero: How a Japanese diplomat saved 6,000 Jews" [January 10, page 9] with its story of the amazing and courageous Japanese diplomat, Chiune Sugihara [a righteous among the nations], and his processing of the visas of thousands of Jews during World War II.)

My hope is that Taiwan could create an award similar to the Israeli prize, recognizing those who have supported and reinforced all that is great about this nation, those who have helped and supported Taiwan on its long journey to self-understanding, freedom, and its own brand of righteousness in world affairs.

Even now there is probably a list of such people who are acknowledged by the people and government of Taiwan, but I do not mean just anyone, not just those who are "Taiwan friendly" or have advocated Taiwan in affable, but often relatively cliché, rah-rah terms about all that is wonderful about Taiwan (any tourist in Taiwan who has enjoyed the people, food, and scenery here would speak up this way).

I mean instead those who have genuinely supported, abetted, and inspired Taiwan, who endorsed change in word and deed, and who have truly embraced and sanctioned the nation's march toward the realization of its democratic polity and commonwealth, which has received its own recognition and acclamation from states and peoples worldwide.

I think that at this point that Taiwan's national awards such as the Order of Blue Sky and White Sun, the Order of Brilliant Star, and the Order of the Cloud and Banner do not quite do the job, and we need something more universal, more inclusive.

Or perhaps this should be a relatively local award, for certainly Taiwan has not undergone anything like what the Jews went through during the Holocaust.

However, this is not to say that Taiwan has not suffered a lot over the years, with its lack of recognition by sister states, its struggle through colonizing and brutal totalitarian regimes, its continued abuse at the hands of China, and the threats directed at Taiwan.

It seems that in many respects, this nation has suffered persecution that has not been altogether different from the worst ravages and aggression that have tormented people in ages past.

And thus, Taiwan needs an accolade, a citation, something recognizing that which is righteous, that which is ethical, honorable, noble, veritably spiritual, virtuous, charitable, and commendable. And to turn outward, perhaps limiting this award only to Taiwan would not be ideal, and the award could be granted to any world citizen who has endorsed and supported the values of democracy, freedom, and human rights in the world today.

This has enlarged this idea a good bit, but I hope something like it can be considered.

One suggestion is Principled Aegis of Common Ethics award. Taiwan, in honoring those who support and defend these qualities and beliefs, can keep pace with the development of universal values in the world today.

With the above said, as an American living in Taiwan, I find the new reality of freedom and self-determination in Taiwan in alignment with my own civic values (and more on this below). The nation has in its way welcomed me, foreigner though I may be. I will discuss this more below in terms of Taiwanese identity. Here I conclude my examination of Taiwan's history, politics, and culture and turn to my next chapter, "Taiwan: Students, Education, and Academia."

CHAPTER 3

Taiwan: Students, Education, and Academia

To be sure my role as an educator in Taiwan has been of primary importance in the last 20 years. I have taught countless classes and innumerable students in dozens of schools and homes, from children to high school students to university classes. As well, I have taught countless others in local businesses, government offices, cram schools, and one-on-one tutoring situations. Much is going on in education in Taiwan, and important changes have been made recently. Notably, a 12-year mandatory educational system has been instituted, which has raised the level of education in Taiwan to international levels. Student scores on international tests have been high, indicating how students can respond well to the best teaching methods (to be examined below).[1] The nation recently organized the 2019 International Conference of Curriculum Leadership for Principals, seeking to facilitate the implementation of the 12-year program, internationalize elementary and secondary schools, and develop curriculum direction. The Ministry of Education has also launched its Life Education

[1] In 2015, Taiwanese students achieved some of the world's best results in mathematics, science, and literacy, in the Programme for International Student Assessment (PISA), a worldwide evaluation of 15-year-old school pupils' scholastic performance. Taiwan is one of the top-performing OECD countries in reading literacy, mathematics, and science, with the average student scoring 523.7, compared with the OECD average of 493, placing it seventh in the world with one of the world's most highly educated labor forces among OECD countries (*Wikipedia*, "Education in Taiwan"). In the QS World University Rankings 2020, National Taiwan University was the top in the country, ranked 69th globally (https://en.wikipedia.org/wiki/National_Taiwan_University).

D. Pendery, *Taiwan—A Light in the East*,
https://doi.org/10.1007/978-981-15-5604-3_3

Middle-Term Project, with the aims of developing life skills and values in young students. I find this to be a very positive development in youth education in Taiwan, perhaps outside of my university focus, but no doubt an important area of research and development (I have written on Life Education before). The Ministry of Foreign Affairs has also launched its Teen Diplomatic Envoys Program, which dispatched a group of teen students to Indonesia and New Zealand in January 2020 "to engage in academic and cultural exchanges with non-governmental organizations and high schools" (*Taipei Times*, January 21, 2020). I quite like this idea. In another important area, Taiwan is seeing a new focus on industry-academia collaboration, which is branching into many new areas of research and development. I am myself participating in one such industry-academia project at this time. Other developments in Taiwan education have been rich and worthwhile, including "exam free" pathways to upper secondary school (more on this below), relaxation of an overly restrictive curriculum (particularly aimed at young students), subsidies for students from disadvantaged homes, support for physically impaired students, improved vocational education, widely available arts education, and the promotion of e-learning.

I have written about my teaching experience in detail in my memoir, *Something Super: Living, Learning and Teaching in Taiwan*. I will not include an excerpt from this work here. Instead, to indicate just where I am and what I feel and do as a teacher, I will share a short piece I constructed that outlines my teaching philosophy. This work has not been published, but I have shared it with some teachers in Taiwan. The following might seem a somewhat personal view, but it can be applied to conceptions of teaching in general and the experience of students in Taiwan. I wrote this when I was a lecturer at Shih Hsin University, a prominent private university in Taiwan.

Teaching Philosophy and Methods

At the highest level, I turn to Aristotle for my approach to teaching and life. Based on his words, I always try to respond to situations at the right times, in the right ways, for the right reasons. In teaching, sometimes this calls for firm or critical treatment of students, while at other times it calls for praise and encouragement. I have responded in these different ways at different times with different students.

When a teacher has some 200 students during the course of a week as I do, it's only natural that there will be some hurt feelings and the occasional negative reaction. I cannot, and will not, be my students' "buddy," or their friendly uncle or their mother or their nanny. Students sometimes need to be reminded of the deep responsibility they have taken on simply by being college students. One of my own responsibilities is to advise students—firmly or gently—that they are obligated to fulfill their responsibilities. There is no gray area here: they either fulfill their responsibilities or they risk disciplinary action. This is all in their best interest and will lead to rewards for them in the future.

The best students tend to respond well to my methods. "You work harder than any other teacher" is a comment I have heard time and again from my students, including here at Shih Hsin. My methods, in addition to the things I have already discussed, include extensive corrections, instruction, and review in English writing and grammar based on modern American English; much detailed practical advice about writing, speaking, and student success techniques based on my own college experience and writing career; multimedia instructional methods, including computer and Internet instruction and communications, and my expertise in a wealth of computerized publishing and writing tools that can help them create better essays, reports, final projects, presentations, and so on; use of modern texts and instructional materials and avoidance of obsolete or obscure writing styles and methods; and an easygoing and often humorous approach that resonates with students (genial laughter is common in my classrooms). Most students have no idea that I am over 40 years old. They see me as one of their own (almost), a casual American man in his late 20s who attended a top American college, who is a skilled writer, and who has designed web pages, been a professional musician, and lived in San Francisco and Boston to boot. This is a significant advantage, as I can reach out to students comfortably, while being able to distance myself from them appropriately.

Negative and rebellious students often tend to view me suspiciously, although they usually come around by the end of a semester. I do not go out of my way to reach these students; I adhere to my path, giving the instruction to all students equally. It is every student's responsibility to absorb and employ my input and suggestions and to not allow immature rebelliousness to affect their performance or intrude during classes. Indeed, I focus my efforts and attention on good students, who deserve to be rewarded with additional attention. Of course, I will speak to problem students when appropriate or necessary and have frequently reached out to them (I have never had a difficult, negative relationship with a student before, although that appears to be changing at Shih Hsin). In the end, the responsibility to succeed and contribute to cooperative classrooms is entirely in students' hands. I will not hold their hands. That is my firm belief.

Up until this semester, I had never failed a single student, so any conception that I am "too hard" or "too strict" is nonsense. If anything, I have been too soft, for I have always gone in the direction of friendly camaraderie with students, rather than a condescending, stiff attitude toward them. I expect mutual respect between teachers and students, energized by hard work and creativity in my classrooms. I expect this of all my students, and I require it of myself. Students have noticed this and appreciate the fact that I treat them as responsible adults, not as children who have to be endlessly pampered. As my friend, a college teacher in San Francisco, once told me: There are two types of teachers. One type treats students as little balls of clay to be shaped and molded according to what the teacher thinks is the best outcome. The other type treats students as seeds who are being tilled into a bit of soil during their college experience and who can be tended in the right ways for the right reasons during this time. These teachers turn the dirt and plant the seeds and apply the water and the fertilizer and then look forward to seeing students thrive in their own directions. I am of the second group.

Although I appreciate the value of fun and a few laughs in the classroom (and as I have said, I frequently accomplish these things), I will not be a comedian in front of my students. We are on a serious educational journey, not a frivolous "four-year vacation." Excellence is a rare accomplishment in life—in school, personal affairs, careers, and so on. Only a small percentage of people (including students) achieve excellence. Excellence is a serious goal that has to be striven for in a serious and committed way. That does not mean we can't have fun on our journey. Half the fun in college is striving and working hard and then producing excellent, intelligent, skillful work that highlights the expertise and creativity of students, which in turn leads to better college performance, blossoming careers, personal satisfaction, and so on. Such accomplishments are not attained through comic, trivial diversions.

This is only a short description of my educational philosophy and beliefs, but I hope it helps you understand who I am and what I try to do.

My experience with students in Taiwan has taken many twists and turns, and I have seen their academic lives up close and personal. I have written on these subjects in academic analyses that have been published in journals worldwide. I will not share any of these works here, but if readers wish they can refer to *Sino-US English Teaching*, the *Journal of Social Change*, the *National Taipei College of Business Journal of Foreign Language and Literature Studies*, the *Selected Papers of the ROC English Teaching Association International Symposium on English Teaching*, or the *Ching Yun Journal of Applied Foreign Language Studies*, for works I have written (Fig. 3.1)

After all of the above, readers might be interested in another view (which in some respects echoes my own). In this respect, I again turn to Dr. Damm, who has taught in Taiwan for many years at very high levels. Dr. Damm jokingly says that education, educators, and students in Taiwan can be "nightmarish" and that there is a lack of critical thinking, too much memorization: "nobody asks for innovation in teaching, very old

Fig. 3.1 One great day teaching in Taiwan

fashioned teaching is prevalent" and "the system is too hierarchical" (common complaints in Chinese education, and this is to say nothing of the rigid test culture that exists here). Martin Jacques writes that in Chinese education, "A high priority is placed on training and technique, as compared with the openness and creativity valued in the West" (199), and this has been observed by many others, and often in Taiwan. More seriously, Damm goes on to criticize "very centralized systems, everything has to be controlled by the Ministry of Education, no real autonomy of universities; a deep mistrust in everybody (a legalist system)." The idea that ancient Chinese legalism—a stark realist system that has been compared to Machiavellianism—could still be impacting educational values and methods today is no doubt a worrisome proclamation (which will be echoed by Professor Ruey-Shiung Chang below). Damm then notes that "Academia Sinica has some great researchers and research attitude" and that some academics in Taiwan "understood that teaching and research requires new ways." "Students are nice" concludes Dr. Damm, "but only a very few dare to challenge their professor." This too is a common lament among foreign teachers in Taiwan.

In terms of the above, and in language that resonates with what Damm has said, I turn to the president of NTUB, Ruey-Shiung Chang (張瑞雄). I interviewed Dr. Chang with my staff writer Eva Chang in November 2019, published in our English newspaper, the *NTUBulletin*.

Professor Chang had his own misgivings about the educational system in Taiwan, telling us that the Taiwan Ministry of Education "has many regulations and 'bondage' with universities and high schools, every level of school has many restrictions. Everything a university wants to do, we have to apply for permission from the MOE. There is a lot bureaucracy." Chang went on that "many Taiwanese high school graduates are going to China, Hong Kong and Singapore for their university degree. They do not stay in Taiwan." Chang added that declining birth rates in Taiwan are adding pressure to universities, as student numbers fall. The birthrate in Taiwan was even called a national security problem by former president Ma Ying-jeou. This may be an overstatement, but to be sure this is a cause of concern. Schools are said to be closing due to a lack of students, but then again, Taiwan always had far too many higher education institutions (there are 141 universities and colleges in Taiwan), with a large number of them of extremely poor quality. With declining birthrates, any number of these schools is having trouble attracting enough students and will be closed, and this has become an important issue here. In Taiwan's history, the very idea of creating as many higher education institutions as possible was long seen as a vital facet of national development and to some extent security. This is now haunting the country in some ways—and I have a feeling Professor Chang would agree. If we trimmed the branches of this tangled system, that would not be a bad idea. These are difficult problems to address and larger social developments faced by many countries today.

Another area of concern is competition from foreign schools (not least Chinese schools). This is a reality that must be squarely faced by Taiwan's higher education, and it must seek to improve the quality of its teaching and research, internationalize its systems, and introduce new talent (much of it foreign talent). This is simply a question of cultivating and developing high-quality education from the bottom up (not the top down) in schools in Taiwan (above taken from the November 26, *NTUBulletin*). In a word, there are a number or problems that Taiwan education now faces.

In a work I wrote about ten years ago (unpublished), I expressed what I hoped was a more positive and constructive view onto teaching in Taiwan than that seen above, borrowing from a work that is of major importance in Chinese culture: the *Dao De Jing*, or *Tao Te Ching* (道德经). This of course is the classic Chinese religious text traditionally credited to the sixth-century BC sage Laozi (老子). I call this piece "The Dao of teaching," and following is a brief excerpt.

The Dao of Teaching

In the following I will examine conceptions of teaching and student life that consider these elements in light of the great teachings in the Dao de Jing (道德經). I believe that the Dao can give excellent guidance for both teachers and students, enabling them to interact in improved ways and achieve success in education.

For my own part, I try to be a modest and practical teacher, crafting my skills to meet student wants and needs, adhering to the purposes of the data being conveyed, and never putting on shows for my students. In a word, I treat my students as plants to be cultivated, similar in the way the Dao advises that "What is firmly established cannot be uprooted" (Book 54), in order to yield excellent and successful students in the future.

Teaching is one of the true social professions, which requires skill in communicating and interacting with others. The interaction in teaching, however, generally takes place on an uneven playing field, with teachers expected to reside "higher" than (lower) students. Perhaps in this respect, we should remember that "High and low rest upon each other" (Book 2) and also that "the high [will be] lowered and the low [will be] raised" (Book 77). Teachers are, I feel, always called on to be good mentors and guides for our students, and we do not need to over-awe them with incredible brainpower and vain displays of sagacity. To turn to the Dao, "Too much success is not an advantage. / Do not tinkle like jade / Or clatter like stone chimes" (Book 39), and we must instead:

> Achieve results,
> But never glory in them.
> Achieve results,
> But never boast.
> Achieve results,
> But never be proud.
> Achieve results,
> Because this is the natural way. (Book 30)

This sounds like a window onto the teaching world, a world in which right and best behavior are constantly called upon, where we must be "good to people who are good," "good to people who are not good" and also "aware of the needs of others" (Book 49).

In one important research study that I conducted in 2013, I looked at happiness levels in Taiwanese students. I think this work can give readers an insightful view into just what is going on with Taiwanese students and even a view into their identity and selves. I based my ideas on the Gross National Happiness level as practiced in Bhutan, as well as the fact that many governments and other institutions are measuring happiness in populations and correlating this with self-actualization, success, and tranquility in life. It may have been that I had noted some indisposition and discontent in my students over the years (not surprising in some respects, given the grueling process of Taiwanese education from primary school on, highlighted not only by the punishing lecture courses taught by indifferent teachers and the mostly hated school entrance examinations [a bugbear throughout Chinese cultures] but also by taxing "cram schools" where students are sent to study for hours additionally every day). I set about work on this paper with the help of a few other teachers and also with the Happiness Alliance, a happiness organization in the United States. I conducted surveys and handed out questionnaires, and my findings were somewhat technical. Rather than my methodological article ("The

Taiwanese Student Happiness Initiative: Fulfilling Lives and Success in the Future," published in the Walden University *Journal of Social Change* in 2015), I will share the following abbreviated article I wrote for the *Taipei Times*, published on October 20, 2014, which relates my findings for a general audience.

Taiwanese Students Not So Happy

I have recently conducted research measuring happiness levels among Taiwanese university students, and from these findings I would like to recommend changes to government and education policies. Measuring happiness in life has become steadily more important in recent years as an indicator of just how people are subsisting and developing, with an eye toward future success and serenity.

Many governments and other institutions are measuring happiness in populations and correlating this with self-actualization, success, and tranquility in life. Even Taiwan has explored these parameters, with the Directorate General of Budget, Accounting and Statistics releasing the nation's first Gross National Happiness index last year. This research found that Taiwanese had a "moderate" level of happiness.

However, what exactly is happiness? In addition to ostensible things like good feelings about life, satisfaction with friends, family, and other relationships, excitement and fun, personal contentment and hope for the future, there are a few other important indicators to consider. External factors include material comforts and income, work satisfaction, vital community relations, decent governance, and access to education, arts, and culture. More personal or internal factors include mental and physical health, rich values and religion, positive family experience, education, gender, and age.

Martin Seligman created the concept of PERMA to measure happiness, which refers to Positive emotions, Engagement in life, Relationships, Meaning in life, and Accomplishments.

As this year's UN World Happiness Report noted, the great thinkers and sages of world history have taught people that "material gain alone will not fulfill our deepest needs. Material life must be harnessed to meet these human needs, most importantly to promote the end of suffering, social justice, and the attainment of happiness."

I conducted my survey measuring happiness factors using an index survey created by the Happiness Alliance, a large happiness organization in the United States. Students from four colleges completed the survey. The data was collected in spring and fall this year, with one multiple sample that initially included 35 students in my culture and communication class at National Taipei College of Business—now National Taipei University of Business (NTUB)—which was increased by 89 more students in a combined group from NTUB and Tamkang University near Taipei in the fall.

Additionally, there were samples from Chien Hsin University of Science and Technology, south of Taipei (26 students), and Shih Hsin University in Taipei (58–64 students). The "domains" measured in the research included satisfaction with life; material well-being; governance; environment; community vitality; social support; access to education, arts, and culture; mental well-being; health; time balance; and work.

In a somewhat disturbing turn, the results showed that the students were not very happy and they scored decidedly lower than worldwide averages on several measures. Interestingly and compellingly, the lowest scores were in the "community" category and the related "social support" category. The figures in the community domain are fully 21–30 points less than the total worldwide average, a difference of 40–57 percent lower. The social support figures are 7–15 percent lower.

To be sure, it is just such community involvement that is essential to a satisfying and contented life. That students are not experiencing this type of connection will sound strange to many, as Taiwan is a land with famously friendly people and student lives are immersed in fun activities with friends.

However, students appear to not be encountering this community involvement deeply. One possibility may be that students' lives are in some senses remote from the communities around them, because they are too busy with schoolwork. A second possibility is that students are spending too much time solipsistically glued to their smartphones.

Schools can step in here and help students to engage locally, by creating programs such as service learning, which connect students to their peers and educators in meaningful ways, and also outward into the community. From this local base, we can reach out globally and encourage overseas volunteer work, which could create globalized communities. This community involvement would provide students with mature, responsible roles in their own neighborhoods and from there into neighborhoods around the world.

At another very high and disturbing level, the results showed that students are feeling less than overall satisfaction with life. My groups had scores lower by 15–26 percent in satisfaction with life and 4–13 percent lower in psychological well-being. The questions in these domains covered overall satisfaction with life, subjective well-being, worthwhile experience, interest in daily activities, and optimism. This is thus an inclusive picture of students' mental lives and just how much they like their existence.

Given that the scores came in so much lower than the world averages, there does appear to be something amiss in Taiwan. One step here could be for schools to instigate programs that show students how to be happier and more comfortable in life. There are probably any number of such programs that could be possible, from the very small—such as one plan that promises happiness simply by first, sitting silently for a few minutes each day; second, practicing gratitude and compassion in life; and third, performing small acts of kindness each day—to larger structured programs—the University of Pennsylvania's Positive Psychology Center, for example, offers syllabi that can be used in semester-long courses. Additionally, schools could become more involved with students' families and contribute in this way.

Two other areas in which students scored lower than global averages were in perceptions of environment and governance. These are areas the central government could step in on, first of all by cleaning up the environment (but again, this is an area that schools could participate in, creating cleanup days and other environmental activities for students) and in general governance.

To be sure, there has been some social upheaval in the nation in recent months and years, and in some senses, young people have taken this problem into their own hands, with large student movements erupting across the country. It is difficult to tell if this will make a difference in the long run, but it is at least true that studies show that people who become active in politics—and enjoy their own freedoms and rights—are happier.

Results in the domain of education, arts, and culture are also low. The findings are fairly substantial—13–23 percent lower than global averages. This is also an area in which schools could step in and enrich students' lives. Introductions to arts and cultural activities, out-of-school performances and museum trips, concerts, literature readings, plays, speeches, field trips, and an ongoing focus on local, national, and global cultures would be of great value in schools.

In terms of education, teachers must commit themselves to new levels of excellence and student enjoyment, cooperation, and response in their classes. To be sure, this is the highest aim for universities, and a new focus and obligation is needed.

We have looked at keys to overall happiness and life satisfaction for students, and these should be addressed by government and schools.

Happiness can be as simple as a "table, a chair, a bowl of fruit and a violin" as Albert Einstein once said, or it can be a lot more, for there are "broader dynamics at play, involving many more countries and deeper trends, with potentially far-reaching implications for people's lives, for social equity and for democratic governance at the local and global levels," as last year's UN Human Development Report says.

Yes, our task is at once local and global—glocal, as is said. Our job is to travel all the paths we can to create richness and greater happiness in all of our lives.

While I am on the subject of happiness, another work I wrote, published in the *Taipei Times* on January 14, 2020, looked at the idea of well-being in Taiwan at large, based on another editorial, "Can nations prosper by putting well-being before GDP?" published in the *Taipei Times* on January 6, 2020. This article considered whether straightforward economics and GDP numbers were the ideal measure of what is best in and for a nation. In the following work I again consider Bhutan and Taiwan's recent numbers in terms of happiness levels of its citizens (which are not too bad). I endorse a "Gross National Happiness" view into society and reject the GDP-focused, anything goes, buccaneer mentality of the economics wild men, which is so common in the United States, particularly. To be sure, this mindset is changing, and "An increasing focus on environmental sustainability, livable cities, holistic health, and fairness and opportunities for all will be a hallmark of economic development in the coming years," as Abdul Abiad, director of the Asian Development Bank's Macroeconomic Research Division, says in this editorial. I am branching away from my look at education here, and this examination can be applied in terms of my look at the future in Taiwan and an understanding of Taiwanese mentality and identity.

Taiwan Could Be a Leader in Well-Being

A Thomson Reuters Foundation article published in the Taipei Times ("Can nations prosper by putting well-being before GDP?" Jan. 6, page 7) presented an idea that I quite like and which might reveal the hardcore liberal, latitudinarian that I am—I have never voted for a single Republican.

I have commented on this in the past, praising Bhutan's move in the 1970s toward a well-being, happiness-oriented society and economy. With Bhutan's focus on psychological well-being, health, education, the nature and management of time, cultural diversity, effective governance, community vitality, ecological diversity, and living standards, all I can say is "Here, here!"

My question here is "Can Taiwan be a leader in this undertaking and its goals?"

Taiwan has been ranked as the happiest country in East Asia and the 25th happiest in the world, according to last year's World Happiness Report; the nation has only become happier in the past few years.

There have also been local surveys examining happiness levels in Taiwan, so the movement is alive in the nation, and I have a feeling that many Taiwanese are indeed thinking of just what these metrics mean as they look at their lives and how they can be more content.

The bottom line is that this is something that people everywhere want—and the whole idea of GDP as a strict measure of everything that is best in a society is being looked down upon more.

With that said, we might turn to an opinion piece by Walter Lohman that was published on the same day ("Accentuate the positive going into the new year," page 6).

In this piece Lohman takes exactly the wrong view and celebrates all that is great about ultra-free markets.

Taiwan, he says, "values markets over state planning, free flow of goods and services over protectionism. This is generally the same in Washington."

To be sure it is, and ever since the Washington Consensus foisted on the world the worst ideas about economic development and planning, the idea of endless privatization, deregulation, slashing government support, and forbidding austerity measures has resulted not only in a seethingly hostile anti-globalization, anti-liberal markets response but also in economic inequality and wealth concentration in the top percentiles of the ultra-wealthy.

Such ideas have for years been largely denounced.

Now admittedly, as the first piece said, "A focus on sustained economic growth has helped raise hundreds of millions of Asians out of poverty," and this will always be important.

Nobody is dismissing the idea of economic prosperity outright, and this model has added to happiness levels everywhere, but this economic planning, in the best sense, very much requires state planning.

So, Taiwan, it is in your hands. Can you make your people happier, more content, comfortable, satisfied with their nation and its governors, and veritably elated with their neighbors and all the people that visit the nation?

Let us hope this is true, and Taiwan can branch away from a draconian, rigid look at economics—the "management of the home," not "make every penny possible and to hell with anyone that disagrees."

To achieve economic success and related levels of contentment, we must "take into account concepts like well-being so that we ensure our economic system is truly aligned with societal goals," as Gemma Corrigan, lead, sustainable markets at the World Economic Forum, said in the first article.

My life as a teacher in Taiwan has been fruitful and rewarding. No doubt there are good reasons to seek education here. The Taiwan Ministry of Education reports that in a survey it conducted, the top three reasons to study in Taiwan were excellent academic resources and quality, diverse culture, and reasonable and affordable tuition. Diversity may be a key here, as fully 10 percent of the students in Taiwan universities and colleges were foreigners in 2018 (*Taiwan News*, February 3, 2019). I have experienced this myself, and courses I have taught at National Taiwan University of Science and Technology have seen a dozen or more students from Indonesia, Vietnam, Malaysia, and China. In some senses, this effort is linked to President Tsai Ing-wen's New Southbound Policy, which aims to broaden exchanges on economic and trade cooperation, talent cultivation, resource sharing, and regional links with SE Asian countries, Australia, and New Zealand. The long-term goal is to create a new type of cooperation based on mutual benefits. And indeed, Taiwan is currently home to more than 500,000 visitors from other Asian countries (Taiwan.gov.tw).

In many ways, I never expected this teaching and education experience, as I was never much of a teacher in my prior life in the United States. No doubt most Western foreigners living in Taiwan do exactly this—teaching English. There are a number of issues and problems associated with this undertaking that I have commented on at times, but will not go into them here. For now, I leave teaching and turn to my next examination, "Identity: Being Taiwanese"—the character, identity, and individuality of Taiwanese, which I find myself brushing close to at times.

CHAPTER 4

Identity: Being Taiwanese

To begin with identity, proper, at one high level I reflected in a letter to the *Taipei Times* on Taiwanese identity, saying that "people in Taiwan are much more varied and profound than the true believers would have us believe, while the nation has been subject to unusual conditions of development, autonomy, government, settlement and cultural development" (January 14, 2008). By "true believers" here I mean the hard-nosed "dictators versus democrats" types, as often as not anti-China zealots. I went on that Chinese history and culture have had a weighty impact on Taiwanese people and their views. I believe I had made this point already, in addition to the impact of various colonizing peoples in Taiwan, and the current impact of many visitors and homemakers from around Asia and the rest of the world in Taiwan. I reject a notion of flattened "Taiwaneseness" as a way to see the people here (though I acknowledge this is their birthright). In the end, I say that "Taiwan, with its amazing variety of communities intersecting with one another, is a country of many ellipses, a contingent, mutable land wherein people can—must—at once retain and pare away essentialist conceptions of race, ethnicity, culture and nationality. In doing this they will discover delightfully robust—thought admittedly decentered—new identities…I may no doubt here sound Utopian, but our challenge may be to combine Taiwan's many identities—the new arrivals, the isolated others, the merchant strangers, the true believers, the assimilated citizens, the angry activists, the proud natives, the disoriented aliens—in a many-hued identity that will evince a fruitful, inclusive,

D. Pendery, *Taiwan—A Light in the East*,
https://doi.org/10.1007/978-981-15-5604-3_4

cosmopolitan transnationality of creative coexistence and combinatory human potential." Enough said! I think I have captured all that *is Taiwanese* (and a whole lot more) with these words. In a related turn, I might add that "Taiwanese have often been characterized as some of the friendliest people in the world" (*Lonely Planet, Taiwan*), and I have in the main discovered exactly this in my life in Taiwan. A Chinese phrase, "人情味" (rénqíngwèi) "human touch" catches this.

Richard Bush and Ryan Hass importantly note that "Taiwan's democratic consolidation over the past 20 years is nothing short of historic and is a definitional feature of many Taiwan residents' identity" (no page number). This is no doubt a key area of Taiwanese self-perception. Professor Jens Damm has commented in these lights in his "Taiwan's Ethnicities and Their Representation on the Internet." In this work, Damm states that "After the period of liberalization and democratization in the late 1980s and 1990s, Taiwan, with a new identity as a postmodern globalized society, started to thrive: There was an increasing emphasis on multiculturalism, and discussions began to take place on how to overcome the rifts between the various ethnic groups in order to create 'a community of 21 million with a shared fate' composed of 'the new Taiwanese', as described by former President Lee Teng-hui" (no page number). Damm goes on that "multiculturalism in Taiwan may be seen as an appropriate tool for bringing together the various ethnic groups in Taiwan and establishing a national identity which is not rooted in the idea of a monolithic ethnic nation."

Professor Damm conducted further research on Taiwanese and their use of the Internet and other technologies and found that "the Internet is helping to foster a global, postmodern and hybrid diaspora, which is leading to an identity formation beyond nationalist and nostalgic yearnings and beyond an ethnic and culturally narrowly defined Chinese/Taiwanese identity" (Damm, 2011, no page number). Damm goes on that "a global, postmodern, and hybrid diasporic Chinese identity" is emerging and that "the…Chinese diaspora is now constantly building links with the various 'Chinese homelands' and overcoming essentialistic and nationalistic forms of identities." There is a touch of techno-babble here, but it is revealing. I have myself written a paper on these basic ideas in terms of Taiwanese students, and a few foreigners I had in a clas in Taiwan, but I will not share this here.

In terms of my own identity and experience living as a mostly non-Chinese-speaking expatriate in an Asian country, as I have said my life has been full of incredible experiences and contours. As part of this experience, and though far from fluent in the language, my study of Chinese has been of paramount importance. Again, this is fully covered in my memoir.

I have deeply immersed myself in my studies of Chinese, and I have enjoyed it immensely. I published an essay in the *Taipei Times* on January 6, 2009, also included in my memoir, *Something Super*, in which I examined my long journey learning Chinese—"The Tears, Joys and Responsibility of Learning Chinese" (January 6, 2009). I found that as I have tunneled deeper into the intricacies of this "promethean" language, it has impacted me in weighty emotional, intellectual, and philosophical ways. "Emotionally, the challenge of studying Chinese has had an impact on my self-esteem and conditioned my interaction with everyone I know," I wrote. I went on that "the fantastic intricacy and enthralling etymologies, orthography and semantics of the characters, the internal diversity of the language, its long history and role in Chinese culture and the straightforward difficulty of trying to cage this dragon could provide a lifetime of intellectual challenge and stimulation." I added that "the very difference of Chinese for Westerners sets up a matrix in which we find ourselves correlating, comparing and counterpoising the two languages and world views—one linear, lettered and Latinate-but-astonishingly-worldly; the other orthogonal, calligraphic and so-Chinese/Asian." I concluded that studying this language was an exceptional responsibility, and through it we contribute to a greater comity, a greater apprehension, and a greater existence for all. It has been an amazing linguistic journey, delving into what is recognized as one of the most storied and deeply historical languages on the planet.

At the highest level, I have experienced a given shift in terms of my own identity in Taiwan—shifting identity is a common enough topic in cultural studies and academia. Certainly, I have experienced changes since moving to Asia, though at times my new US/Taiwan identity is simply more of the same—the similarities between the two polities and Taiwan's wide adoption of Western values yield this (to be sure the notions of constitutional government, rule of law, free elections, and an independent judiciary, so engrained in Taiwanese life, point to this). Related to this, you could say that political polarization is similar in both countries, as in some respects I have examined. Many Americans value the fact that they share a language, customs, values, religious beliefs, political views, and historical memory (though to be sure a "shared language" in the United States is less actual than ever; tens of millions of Americans speak Spanish at home, which I have seen growing up in New Mexico, and this is to say nothing of the many other languages spoken in the United States). To some extent this is true in Taiwan, though there is no particular "Chinese Only" movement in Taiwan compared to "English Only" in the United States (supporters of this movement in the United States decidedly *do not* want to "share language values" with others). It has been proposed to make English a second official language in Taiwan (bringing my culture and Taiwanese culture that much closer), though that is probably years in the future (to be sure the majority of major politicians in Taiwan speak English even now; I have also found that virtually every doctor here can speak English reasonably well; my experience with students has been that their English is "not bad," though you often see articles criticizing Taiwanese students and claiming their English is not very good). I have considered other aboriginal languages spoken in Taiwan above.

In many of these respects it has been said that Americans view their country as a promised land, a shining city on a hill, where a people looking for freedom can find refuge. Taiwanese people would not disagree with this, though they have never been able to actually see their country as precisely this, and to this day the shadow of immense and illustrious Chinese culture—a Middle Kingdom that most assuredly has its positive aspects, but has always been burdened with a given mercenary and to some extent predatory tendency (forgive me if this sounds strong)—has been viewed in part in this light (now my "shadow" has become a "light"). America is a country that largely values diversity and immigration, and the same could be said for Taiwan, which as noted has large foreign populations. Finally, America is a very modern country, and in some ways anti-traditional, anti-Old World, anti-European (in spite of the nation's roots in these cultures). Taiwan is to be sure a very modern land, but this view may differ here with its connection to traditional Chinese culture (which is both valued and dismissed in Taiwan) and in its general communitarian ethic (as opposed to American individualism).

Taiwan: A city on a hill. Not a few foreigners have come to Taiwan for just this reason, and thus there is something of a similarity to United States' values and its vaunted dreams. I examined this reality in the following editorial published in the *Taipei Times* on April 2, 2019. This work says much about what the Taiwanese identity really is and how it is realized and functions—if in somewhat political terms.

Taiwan a "City on a Hill" for Asia

I have written about Taiwan in past editorials in the *Taipei Times* and usually enunciated political/social arguments about Taiwan independence, the two main political parties, identity in Taiwan, threats to Taiwan from abroad, the nation in world affairs, Taiwan's history, its military, and so on. In this piece I would like to step back a bit and compose a more reflective piece (though politics in Taiwan is never far behind). In some senses this is an "identity" piece and also a work about Taiwan's role, character, and attributes in world affairs.

Here I am viewing Taiwan from a high level, and from this perspective I am bestowing on Taiwan what I think is a meaningful characterization, which authentically captures the nation's essence. This is that I see this land, in John Winthrop's words, as a "city on a hill" in Asia, a beacon of freedom and democracy that speaks to its neighbors and all other nations around the world that "we shall be made a story and a by-word through the world." Here and below I will take from Winthrop's "A Model of Christian Charity" speech to the New England Puritan immigrants he had traveled across the Atlantic with in 1630.

The word city originates from the Latin for "citizen," and certainly such a designation is important in Taiwan, with its autonomous and sovereign citizens, ensconced in a free republic. In turn, the picture of the city being "on a hill" denotes a viewpoint and frame of reference (that of Taiwan's citizens, their attitudes and opinions, their suffrage, their franchise), a prospect and panorama of the autonomous nation.

I warrant that Taiwan can now be viewed as this city on a hill in Asia, and indeed, "the eyes of all people are upon [Taiwan]." I should probably say here, the eyes not least of China, which sees Taiwan as this beacon, this light shining in a sometimes benighted part of the world, inspiring peoples and nations everywhere with its somewhat modest (democracy, plain and simple), but oh so multifaceted polity. Here, in a word, we find that "every man might have need of others, and from hence they might be all knit more nearly together." Taiwan has exhibited such binding and attachment to peoples and countries all over the world, most apparently and creditably in its aid, funding, and cooperative work with other nations in areas of agriculture; medicine and public health; education; transportation, logistics, and construction; "people to people" communications; women's rights; environmental protection; humanitarian assistance and disaster relief; and technical development. In some respects, Taiwan has even treated China this way, such as with the aid to the victims of the 2008 Sichuan earthquake in China, which benefited many people. Additionally, the Taiwan Fellowship provides for research into this area of the world, connection with opinion leaders worldwide, academic relations and internationalization of education, and cultural and public diplomacy. All of these efforts in part focus on China and the PRC's relations with Taiwan.

In another important way, Taiwan's multidimensionality is seen in the many peoples and cultures that live or are educated here. To be sure foreigners from everywhere are choosing to make Taiwan their home (this writer is a prime example of this), and the multiculturalism that Taiwan evinces, the variety of languages and cultures that are enthusiastically advocated and embraced, is a joy to everyone who makes their domicile here.

These are only some elements of the whole story, and the more important facet is (again) a good bit more "political." On the one hand, as Winthrop said, Taiwan is something of a "community of peril" (in Taiwan we would say "in peril"). Here again the nation must "knit" itself with others, "uphold a familiar Commerce together," and disseminate "Commission and Community…our Community as members of the same body, so shall we keep the unity of the spirit in the bond of peace." Here Taiwan's own allies are of utmost importance, as are its relationship to the United States, Japan, the EU, Australia, and many other smaller nations around the world. Political and military arrangements are vital, as are those "people to people" connections mentioned above, and also economic agreements, which provide sustenance, enable growth, and provide the means for aid and support. In this light, the forthcoming Trans-Pacific partnership is significant, as is cooperation with the APEC nations. These are areas Taiwan must focus on.

Though military cooperation is imperative, Taiwan has, in light of this, much more importantly endeavored in peaceful international collaboration for years and years and has never made a single hostile or aggressive move toward any other nation around it. Some say Winthrop's words are reminiscent of the Sermon on the Mount, with a focus on benevolence and agreement. In these ways Taiwan seeks to "see much more…wisdom power goodness and truth" and to bring these qualities to its friends and neighbors (and even to its enemies, few though they are). In terms of any "threats" that Taiwan might face in these respects, China is of course at the fore here, and answers have been frustratingly difficult to fashion. At this point, one hopes that we really are family across the Taiwan Strait.

Another angle may be a focus on "pleasures, and profits," which it is hoped do not distract the nation from its greater good and goals. I think Taiwan has been somewhat guilty in this regard, with a focus on a somewhat mercantile approach to economic growth.

To be sure the conception of the "city on a hill" is central to American culture and identity. Could the same be true for Taiwan? Why not? Because the truth is that Taiwan is such a hillside city in Asia, an empire of liberty, an exceptional example of a nation with a unique and deep-running historical memory, a "first new nation" (the phrase is from Seymour Martin Lipset) based on liberty, egalitarianism, republicanism, and democracy (and, we should probably add, laissez-faire economics, though this introduces difficulties). Taiwan, be it known—and almost everyone around the world does know this—an inspiration to freedom-loving people in Asia and the world.

To "become Taiwanese" in my way has not always been easy. It has been a bumpy road, chock full of culture shocks and, in some respects (such as not speaking Chinese fluently), less than successful (though quite a few people have commented to me that my Chinese is excellent, a number of others have looked askance at my less than complete command of the language). My American identity differs in some respects from those of Taiwanese, though as noted in other ways it is very similar. In a work I include below, "Tombs are not for the dead," the reader will see a hint of my new identity shining through in my interaction with my wife's family members.

In terms of actual identity here, at the highest level I have considered obtaining actual citizenship in Taiwan, which in the past was not possible. Cold War and authoritarian restrictions required anyone who desired this to rescind their home citizenship, something I would never consider. This harsh limitation put Taiwan in a select group of inflexible and restricted countries (dictatorships as often as not) and expunged it from membership in the company of truly free countries in the world, where dual citizenship is perfectly common. Taiwan in this way was not the open, progressive, equitable, and free nation it claimed to be.

However, I discovered this was in fact possible in Taiwan, when I saw an article in the *Taipei Times*, describing how a change in law here would allow citizenship to be available to a select group of foreigners in Taiwan (the requirements are quite stiff, and a high level of professional accomplishment is required; the *Taipei Times* has now reported on up to 150 foreigners who have achieved this, including priests who have lived here for decades and speak local languages fluently and who have opened hospitals and schools, a few educators, an American basketball player, a Turkish soccer coach, and others). This reality has opened a new door of dual nationality in the world and, in my eyes, has created the opportunity for foreigners in Taiwan to achieve a kind of "world citizen" status.

I ultimately encountered this reality in a new way, when my daughter was born in 2016. Simply put, little Ariadne does indeed have dual citizenship. Needless to say, with an American father she automatically has US citizenship, and with a Taiwanese mother, the same is true for Taiwan. Our hope now is that she will be fully bilingual and at home and comfortable in both cultures.

I considered all of these issues in a letter published in the *Taipei Times* on July 4, 2017, in which I lamented the reality that citizenship seemed out of reach for the average foreigner in Taiwan.

Taiwanese Dreams Quashed

I have learned a hard lesson about Taiwanese life and politics, which indicates that this is not the open, progressive, equitable, and free nation it claims to be.

About six months ago, I learned that Taiwan had changed its laws and was allowing foreigners to become citizens. This was hardly possible in the authoritarian past when one was required to give up one's home citizenship before being able to become a Taiwan citizen.

This harsh limitation put Taiwan in a select group of inflexible and restricted countries (dictatorships as often as not) and expunged it from membership in the company of truly free countries in the world, where dual citizenship is perfectly common.

When I found out about this law change, I was very excited. I hoped that I could have a chance to gain Taiwanese citizenship.

I saw there were various requirements that did restrict the possibility of citizenship and in some ways this right was limited to fairly high-level professionals in various fields, but I felt I could meet the standards. I have lived and paid taxes in Taiwan for 17 years, have entirely relocated here, and now say this is my home and will be until the day I die. I have contributed to culture here in many ways, not least in the fact that I have coached and taught and trained thousands of students in Taiwanese schools, from children to college students.

I have not been truly active in Taiwan politics, but I am fully aware and expert in all that Taiwan experiences and faces politically in the world, and have at times spoken publicly on these issues (including in the *Taipei Times*).

I am an associate professor who has published dozens of academic papers, a certain high-level status in education.

Yes, I felt that I was far from just any foreigner breezing through Taiwan for a few years, teaching in cram schools and boozing it up at foreigner bars five nights a week. I have lived a sober and committed life here, for going on two decades.

This said, I attempted to look into the possibility of citizenship. I knew by this time you could not just pop into any government office and apply. You had to have approval at a fairly high level.

So I went to the president of my school, Ruay-shiung Chang of the National Taipei University of Business, and got a letter of recommendation from him. I thought this should pretty much be enough to get started, but I was very wrong.

When I tried to submit this to Taipei's Yonghe District city office, I was told brusquely: "No way, it is not good enough; you need a letter from the highest level of Taiwan government."

This meant the Ministry of Education.

Well, this was disappointing and it was made worse by the woman in Yonghe telling me in no uncertain terms: "Nobody is going to get this; you have to be a Catholic priest who has lived in Taiwan for 50 or 60 years; nobody else will obtain citizenship."

Indeed, the only foreigners who have thus far gained Taiwanese citizenship (about five people) are Catholic priests [and nuns] who have lived here for four or five decades.

This was all worrisome, but I pressed on. I returned to the school president and asked if he could go to the Ministry of Education.

He said he would try.

To make a long story short, several weeks later he told me: "No chance, they said they will not do it."

It turns out the woman in Yonghe was right and no other foreigners are receiving this right and privilege in Taiwan (I have heard of no others, even teachers who have been in Taiwan 40 years and more).

When I got this news, the game was up and I knew I had no chance of ever obtaining Taiwan citizenship, a right and privilege I had looked forward to in the most faithful and determined ways.

I wanted to give back (to vote on issues and candidates in the future), to contribute politically, socially, and personally, to this nation which has given so much to me.

However, I found out that Taiwan will give so much, but no more.

And so I saw the truth. Taiwan is not the tolerant, leading-edge, egalitarian place it loftily claims to be. It is far from that. It is still a polity lodged in black, Cold War, autocratic politics that limits freedoms, rights, and benefits.

I hoped for something greater, Taiwan, but it was not to be. I will go on living here as I have for some decades, but I will never be "Taiwanese," as I once dreamed.

In one respect, I made an entry into Taiwanese governance (not quite "citizenship") when I obtained a Taiwan driver's license in 2015. This was an almost-amusing process—some could call it that, though for me it was steeped in frustration. What was "funny" was that I required fully five tests at a driving track in Taipei before I succeeded and was awarded the license (I had even practiced once on a practice track, and the man there said "Looks good, I think you'll make it"). On the test track you drive a car; navigate various turns, rises, starts, and stops in the vehicle; park the car; perform parallel parking; drive in reverse; cross a railroad track; and the like. I found that I sometimes made slight errors, such as not using the turn signal when exiting a parked area (I would normally think that is not even necessary), and found that you were only given about two such mistakes, after which they promptly announced that the test was over, and you had failed. After the fourth time this had happened, I was on the verge of giving up, but tried one more time—and made it through. After reversing the car and entering and exiting a parallel parking test, without bumping the curb, I thought I had it made; I almost did, though toward the end of the test, I stalled the car while entering a pedestrian crossing, and they announced "That's ten points off, continue." I made it to the end of the test, and in a near gasp asked the tester, in Chinese, "Did I make it?" He answered in Chinese, and I just understood that I had. I was still a nervous wreck, but when I entered the administration area and began to make my way through, I saw it happening, and they handed me my driver's license. I was "Taiwanese" in a new way then (I later asked a man in the subway, in English, "Is this a Taiwan driver's license?"and he informed me (in English) that it was). I have driven minimally here, but it was handy to have the associated international driver's license when I returned to the United States.

Having a driver's license to drive might seem a relatively unimportant point in terms of politics and culture, but in fact these permits are relatively important on the world stage, and many states do not recognize those of other countries, thereby refusing to recognize a given state's sovereignty. Many countries in the world, including the United States, do not recognize Taiwanese drivers' licenses (a few US states do).

Though unsuccessful in some respects as I have described, in other ways I have been very successful adapting to the culture in Taiwan—not surprising after living here for 20 years. I have considered the parameters of this experience (and oh how varied and deep they are) and written it up in a piece published in the *Taipei Times* on January 3, 2018.

On Being a Foreigner in Taiwan

As a foreigner in Taiwan—we the waiguoren (外國人)—I face a host of challenging contingencies, complications, and conundrums every day. No doubt language use is at the top of my concerns, and the trial and effort of studying and attempting to use Chinese is a daily concern.

After years of study—I have been nothing if not diligent in my industry—my Chinese is passable. I have sweated over my books and other materials for hours at a time, struggled to speak the language, and labored over reading and writing this devilishly intricate language—writing, in spite of the difficulty, has always been my strong point.

I communicate in the language every day now and often construct complete sentences and dialogues, which pleases me immensely.

However, despite my progress, I have to admit that I am less than fluent—which, alas, is usually the sine qua non for actually being able to steer your way in a new culture using a new language.

The differences separating Chinese from English are a true gulf. The language's parsing, calligraphy, nuance, orthography, and syntax are at times mystifying. I simply do not think in terms of characters that carry entire chunks of meaning (I like little slips of writing—letters—to formulate meaning in an essentially linear fashion); the constant repetition in Chinese is cumbersome; the identical sounds are confounding (foreigners studying here probably know that Chinese people can hear a sentence that says ma mamamama (麻媽罵馬嗎) and it can be understood as a coherent sentence; there is no corresponding "I, I, I, aye, I, I, eye, I" in English); tonal differentiation is a major struggle (we have "stress" in English, but it is a far cry from the four or five tones in Chinese); and I ponder what looks to me like a veritable lack of any grammar (it all seems to be a mass of usages, apothegms, and habitudes).

Any foreigner studying Chinese in Taiwan knows exactly what I am talking about.

Additionally, there is the task of accommodating oneself to a new culture, in this case a very Chinese and/or Confucian culture. Again the differences loom.

Many observers have commented on this in the past, often lobbing criticisms at Confucian culture, which is considered outmoded, archaic, limiting of free thought and critical inquiry, and politically disingenuous.

Chinese Confucius Institutes worldwide, seemingly innocuous cultural institutions and a "soft power" move by China, represent "a serious threat to freedom of thought and speech in education" the BBC wrote on December 22, 2014.

Yutang Jin, a master's student at Hertford College, wrote in 2016 of the "discrimination and injustice that women face in Confucian societies today."

Herbert Hanreich, an assistant professor in Taiwan, called Confucian filial piety downright "immoral" in the *Taipei Times* ("Filial piety is an immoral concept," Oct. 25, 2017, page 8).

I might not come down this hard, but the vagaries and dissimilarities between Taiwanese and Western arts and culture are at times a bit awkward.

In terms of art, it is up and down. Local photography and cinematography have shown promise, with artists like Chi Po-lin (齊柏林), Ang Lee (李安), and a number of other directors having had a significant impact in film.

In terms of music, due to the art form's universal values and skill sets, I will not comment at length—there are plenty of good Taiwanese musicians.

However, in a larger view I might look at the National Symphony Orchestra, and its venue the National Concert Hall, and see this as world-class—and there is a cultural connection. Taiwanese folk music, always closest to the hearts of local people, seems not to have reached true global status and recognition, compared with US folk music. This might be a cultural disconnect with me.

Putting aside the likes of classical Chinese art in the National Palace Museum (a different category, and obviously venerated worldwide), local arts like Taiwanese opera and puppetry have never been to my taste, I find them too traditional. I am perhaps again disconnected from local culture in this way.

Further, I find that Taiwan has no real modern art movement of its own, and current works borrow heavily from Western styles, thus removing much in the way of "Taiwanese-ness."

Looking at the local culture, night markets and temple affairs are pleasing in their ways, but tend toward the tawdry.

However, have you noticed the way aged Taiwanese rise at 4 am and go to the parks to practice taichi, chant, cycle, and exercise? I might not be there yet, but that looks good to me—there is a connection.

At a higher level, the somewhat nonchalant—many say careless—treatment of the environment here has been an ongoing problem. Business and vocational life have been quite successful, but have been accused of unscrupulous behavior.

Meanwhile, Taiwanese politics seems a bit less than genuinely skilled and practiced. Love or hate US president Donald Trump, he (and former US presidents Barack Obama, George W. Bush, and Bill Clinton) knows the game in ways that President Tsai Ing-wen (蔡英文) could never match.

In these terms, although I have done my best to fit in, interact, and function within the culture at large in Taiwan, at times things are still rather "foreign" to me.

However, despite this, some say I indeed seem to have transformed myself into a Taiwanese entity after being here as long as I have—and I too sometimes feel as much, if in a once-removed way. I am not sure that I have taken the final step, though, and gaps remain.

In the big picture, I am not truly there yet, certainly not in terms of possessing any true identity outside the one noted on my US passport. My Taiwanese resident certificate is nice, but it is less than the "real deal."

I have discussed my pursuit of the "real deal"—Taiwanese citizenship—in another forum. I suspect just this might happen someday, when the government opens its eyes to the necessity and morality of dual citizenship. I will welcome that day.

Any disconnects aside, I try to conform and harmonize in my interface and collaboration with the good people of this nation. This is rewarding in its own right and on the whole my life here has been much better than my life in the United States ever was.

I absolutely love it here. In this respect, I am the real deal, I am fully affianced and involved in life here. Is that all that is required? Very possibly yes, for to love a place is to adopt it, to receive it, to embrace it, to take it as one's own, to "be" it—even to the point of possessing its identity.

You are not a "foreigner" any longer; you are one of the people, as best you can be. Such a feeling this nation and its populace have provided me.

Taiwanese have welcomed me, embraced me, accepted me. For that I give thanks—and in the future, my friends, I will "be Taiwanese" in every way that I can.

In terms of the above-mentioned citizenship, I commented in a letter I published in the *Taipei Times* on February 20, 2020, looking at aspects of citizenship and the idea of nation as well as the ways in which these privileges are effected and lived by citizens. These points have very much been seen in Taiwan's citizens, who have become ever more engaged in local and international politics and policies in the last many years.

Nationality Is Absolute

A recent editorial ("Beware closing doors to free speech," February 16) discussed flag burning and the impact this can have in communities and the privilege or right to perform such an action within a nation-state.

The editorial started by citing University of Malaysia researcher Helen Ting, who wrote that the conception of a nation in the world is "a mental construct," and national identity is "a dynamic, contentious historical process of social construction." Ting went on that citizens of nations conceive of a "figured world of nationhood," fashioned within a conception of "socially constructed activities." This is all "only one of many figured worlds that constitute the self" the editorial went on.

This all strikes me as post-modern/deconstruction theoretical babble and ignores realities of nationhood that are important in everyone's life. This is all related to Benedict Anderson's Imagined Communities (also referred to in the editorial), which, while in some ways a useful concept, misses the bar of what nationhood and nationality actually are. That is, my nation—my "community" if you will—is not some sort of mental construct, pie-in-the-sky, floating-in-air, abstract, make-believe conception for me. I live in my community, exercise my rights there, interact with my neighbors, contribute locally, work, play, and relax there. It is not some fictional "construct" much less a "figured world"; it is the real thing. It is indeed "conspicuous" in my life, in my heart, creating a sense of pride (low key in its way), and I see myself very much as a flesh-and-blood American, with all that that means. See my "Taiwan a 'city on a hill' for Asia" in the *Taipei Times* for more on this (April 19, 2019).

The editorial then looks at flag burning, proper. At the highest level, I can understand how this seems offensive to some people, but I would not in the least endorse banning it—such an action is just what has been said in major court rulings in the US Supreme Court—protected free speech. The editorial then claims that the flag represents "group memberships and strong emotional attachments" and, further, embodies "the soul of a society in terms of symbolic representation of national consciousness." I won't disagree that flags are strong symbols and in a sense represent a nation's core values, but these ideas in the main veer into more psycho-gibberish. We American's don't walk around all day pondering the stars and stripes and just how they symbolize the original 13 colonies, the 50 states, valor, purity, perseverance, and justice. Yes, I had to recite the Pledge of Allegiance every morning in school as a child, but that eventually drifted away, and the flag did not linger in my mind every day of my life. I don't think I or anyone I knew was seeing red, white, and blue all day; we were not "waving the flag" at every opportunity. There were realities to attend to, processes that included actual rights and privileges, which I enjoyed and practiced every day—not a world of red, white, and blue symbolism and "constructions," which is imagined, fancied, veritably fictionalized.

The editorial concludes by stating "There is no definitive answer as to whether people should be allowed to desecrate national symbols." This may be true, but there is a definitive answer to what it means to be a citizen of a nation. We are representatives as it were, believers in values, aborigines and commoners, subjects of a greater body politic, voters and delegates, emblems of a nation, a community, a state and a commonwealth. The commonwealth—here is a conception that is anything but imagined; it is lived, it is acquiesced to and abided by, it is breathed, and it is actuated. That is anything but "imagined."

In another look at identity, Taiwan enacted a law in 2019 that has had great impact. Here I refer to Lesbian-Gay-Bisexual-Transsexual-Queer (LGBTQ) people and how they are often choosing nowadays to identify themselves in ways different from what was expected when they were born. Some are even choosing "no identity" by stating that they in fact have no gendered self. Most importantly, their identity in terms of their selves is vital in terms of who they choose to partner with and ultimately marry. In 2019 Taiwan became the first country in Asia to legalize same-sex marriage with the Enforcement Act of Judicial Yuan Constitutional Interpretation No. 748. Taiwan now provides all the ordinary rights and privileges attached to being legally married for LGBTQ people. The law was met with great excitement in Taiwan and Asia and from there had an international impact. This was seen as a major development in global human rights, and Taiwan can be proud to have made an impact here.

I have myself investigated these themes, covering the Taiwan Gay Pride Parade in November 2019 for my *NTUBulletin* English newspaper. The theme for this year's parade was "Together, Make Taiwan Better," and it was believed that more than 200,000 visitors from around the world attended. This reporter met an amazing array of international participants, from Tokyo, Taiwan, the United States, Germany, Turkey, and Norway. "This is forbidden in Turkey," said Lijun, of Turkey. "It should be free, free to live. No government can stop it." Sean, a mental health counselor from the United States, said "I'm here to support the community. As a counselor, I am happy to have friends and family in the LGBT community. It's a misunderstood community and this is unprecedented. It's very warm and welcoming." Eric Chen, a gay man of Taiwan, said "We are here to prove ourselves. Taiwan is a free country with human rights. The pluralism…it's more inclusive and friendly than other countries." And finally, Cecilia Peterson of Norway said that "This is the only country in the region where this is recognized. Marriage is legally recognized here and this has inspired other countries." All of these comments indicate how Taiwan has separated itself from all of Asia with its laws and recognition of basic human rights and placed itself in league with major countries worldwide that see life this way. However, Taiwan may be somewhat conflicted here, as in referendums in Taiwan in 2018, the public rejected a marriage equality proposal and also that a wider array of sexual conduct and preference should be taught to young students. They in turn supported a referendum that defined marriage as a union between one man and one woman.

To conclude my thoughts here about roles and expectations that foreigners must wrestle with living in Asia, in a letter to the *Taipei Times* on June 13, 2008, I pointed out the following efforts we should all be making as we create homes in a new culture:

1. Endeavor to become more competent in the culture and language so that we can become better contributing citizens.
2. Try to reach out to more and create social and/or professional outlets to interact in.
3. Be the best we can be—cooperative, enthusiastic, friendly, and optimistic—in order to raise the bar and show that we foreigners in Taiwan are okay, after all.

I will now turn to one piece that describes my life and experience in Taiwan in a more intimate way. This is more of a leisure/travel piece, written as a feature in the *Taipei Times*, published on May 17, 2015. Once again, I have covered all of my travels and leisure in Taiwan in my memoir. I have traveled with good friends and family all over the island, to remote environments, gorgeous resorts, amazing hot springs, beautiful sandy beaches, towering mountain ranges, delightful seaside villages, aboriginal hamlets, booming cities with amazing cultural features and attributes, and on and on. The following piece is a personal piece about family relations during Tomb Sweeping Day, a holiday shortly after Chinese New Year, during which Chinese people honor their dead and clean their grave sites. This kind of interaction, much of it with distant relatives of my wife who I hardly know, is some of the weightiest experience I have had in Taiwan, touching filial relations (though not actually my immediate family) in deep ways. I often speak a few words of Chinese at such gatherings, which always brings a strong positive reaction (it is always best to speak the native language of the country you are visiting or live in). During rituals like this I feel as I have often felt in Taiwan—the feeling of being a newfound person in a unique culture, surrounded by an unfamiliar dialect, and immersing myself in new, sometimes strange, always enthralling experiences and cultural impressions. None other than Nando Parrado, a survivor of the harrowing 1972 rugby team plane disaster in the Andes Mountains, said something in his classic book, *Miracle in the Andes*, that seems to impel me in these directions. I recently finished this book, a masterwork that describes this experience in deeply emotional and touching ways. The book changed my life, and thus very much became a part of my own identity going forward. I have communicated with Mr. Parrado, and expressed my feelings to him. In the book, Mr. Parrado wrote:

> I did feel something larger than myself, something...that, in rare moments, reassured me, and made me feel that the world was orderly and loving and good. If this was God, it was not God as a being or a spirit or some omnipotent, superhuman mind. It was not a God who would choose to save us or abandon us, or change in any way. It was simply a silence, wholeness, an awe-inspiring simplicity. (263)

This, at some level, reflects my amazing new life and spirit and the ambiance that surrounds me in this amazing new land. Following is "Tombs are not for the dead."

Tombs Are Not for the Dead

I am an American who has lived in Taiwan for 15 years, and I have had lots of evocative experiences during this time. My problem is where to begin? I have related my story in my book *Something Super: Living, Learning and Teaching in Taiwan*, which was kindly reviewed by this paper. So I have told most of my tales of teaching, interacting with students, learning language, participating in Taiwanese politics, going to school, volunteering, and the like.

For this piece, I would like to focus on a small event that occurred a few weeks ago. This event, as many others I have attended in Taiwan, was a mixture of both cultural inspiration and a dose of culture shock.

On that day, I traveled with my Taiwanese wife to Miaoli, to the south of Taipei to participate in a tomb sweeping activity. This was slightly different from the normal Tomb Sweeping Day (清明節)—not only did it take place two weeks after the end of the Lunar New Year (a day chosen out of convenience for some participants), but it was also seen through a Hakka cultural lens, as opposed to the normal Chinese festivity.

The weather that day was fine, and visitors to Taiwan are familiar with the pleasant green setting in Miaoli. We arrived carrying a heavy load of foodstuffs, to be placed around the tombs of my wife's great-grandfather, grandfather, and grandmother. Upon arriving I was the only foreigner in the crowd, which always sets the participants tittering and talking under their breath—politely of course. Soon, I was overhearing my name, and "David's doing…" (大為在做。。。) and "David said…" (大為說。。。) sifted through the group. I didn't attempt to speak much Mandarin and I regretted this, but everyone was perfectly nice to me.

The tombs were located in almost remote areas in the hilly locale. I observed and participated in all of the funerary rites with grave respect, immersing myself in this cultural awakening. I took part in the principal prayer ritual twice with my wife and once with one of her relatives. "Baibai" (拜拜) is phrase you hear over and over again at tomb sweeping, and people pray in order from oldest to youngest. We stood before the graves and bowed three times. This process was then repeated three times. We were asked to splash a small glass of alcohol onto the gravestones, which was done in order to placate the dead.

The rituals took place in two principal spots: at the grave of the deceased person and a small Earth God stone nearby, which guards the grave. Masses of incense were lit, and I found myself holding four or five sticks at a time and giving them back to the hosts as prayers were recited. These were in turn stuck into the ground near the headstones.

As is often the case, the first two graves were large structures with semicircular yard areas in front. A leaf of yellow paper money under a stone is placed on top of each grave, which identifies it as actually housing a deceased person, rather than an empty site. Foodstuffs were placed around the front, and particularly the chicken (with the head of course), pork, and fish must be placed in exactly the right positions. As the relatives walked about, I noted that a few people seemed to be sweeping the area and I wished I could locate a broom to do my part.

The culture shock hit when we arrived at the third and final grave, that of my wife's grandmother. I saw that the cemetery was covered in thick weeds and paper money was scattered around on the graves, as part of the ritual. This made me uncomfortable. My wife later explained this was because the cemetery was not truly permanent, but a "temporary" grave site where people are buried and left to decompose for a few years, before their remains are gathered and transferred to permanent locations. So her grandmother, who was located under nothing more than a mound of earth in this cemetery, would soon be transferred to the tomb of her husband up in the hills.

Throughout these ceremonies I felt a feeling I have often felt in Taiwan—being a new person in a new culture, surrounded by a new language (though I can hardly call Mandarin "new" any more), and baptizing myself in new, sometimes strange, usually fascinating, always enlightening ceremonies, rituals, and cultural patterns.

I am sure almost every foreigner in Taiwan would agree that this is one of the joys of life overseas. At times it can be troubling, but even small events like this one are windows into something grand, edifying, and uplifting—something we expatriates know, which few of our own relatives back home can ever experience.

Steinbeck said it well, and his words open my eyes to all I have experienced in Taiwan: "A kind of light spread out from her. And everything changed color. And the world opened out. And a day was good to awaken to. And there were no limits to anything."

Light, color, a new world, an awakening, no limits. That has been my life in Taiwan, right down to the little things.

In a final look at my thoughts and feelings about the culture and polity of Taiwan and their self-image, I will include a work published in the *Taipei Times* on July 3, 2019. The work captures a feeling I have for this nation at a political level, a feeling which has absorbed me for many years and is in fact a core reason why I like it so much here as a foreigner adapting to a new life in Asia. This work examines Taiwan in a broader light, looking at the roles and place of the nation in the world as a transnational state. The transnational state claim views the state as transforming in the twenty-first century (though the term originated early in the twentieth century with progressive writer Randolph Bourne), with increased linkages among peoples, and declining economic and social significance of boundaries among classic nation-states. The idea crosses politics, economics, and perhaps most importantly socio-cultural factors, including migration into countries and the new peoples and hyphenated "others" that commonly reside in countries today.

Transnationalism is driven by the above-mentioned immigration and new technologies that have made transportation and communication widely available and inexpensive. This has substantively changed the relationship between peoples and states (or simply "places," which is how states are now seen). Simply put, it is now possible for immigrants in new lands to maintain closer and more frequent contact with their home nations, connecting "places" worldwide.

Additionally, global political transformations and new international legal regimes have weakened the state as the only legitimate source of rights. Decolonization, the fall of communism, international diasporas, and the ascendance of human rights as a primary factor in national affairs have all required states to view citizens in new, more accommodating lights. Taiwan has been at the forefront of these developments and has a truly transnational population with citizens from all over the world residing here and many even taking on Taiwanese citizenship proper. In sum, this is a generous, cooperative world view that sees people as people and more than simply "nationals" or even citizens of the state.

Taiwan Is a True Transnational State

The transnational state is a relatively new conception in global affairs (though it originated in the early twentieth century), which posits that heightened interconnectivity is reducing the significance of economic, political, and social borders between individuals, states, and other groups, while increasing communication and connection between all parties. In a word, transnationalism refers to manifold links and relationships, correspondent cultural filaments, coupling people and institutions across the borders of nation-states.

Some might confuse "globalization" with transnationalism, but the global view tends to be more centered on economics, while that which is "trans-" is just that—going across, through, changing. The transnational is more aligned with identity, individuality, and from there, how such uniqueness is positioned in the truly communal (some also speak of historical elements in the transnational, that is, how fluctuations within the history of one country are impacted by developments in others).

At one high level, Kwame Anthony Appiah has spoken of a responsibility to learn from differences. This is a point we should all take to heart. I've said it before: As a foreigner living in Taiwan I have been thrust into a new world of difference, and as a certain "other" in this country, I am yet more obliged to make a difference of my own in my interaction and collaboration with the Taiwanese people. I will do my best, and may we all. And I've said this before too: Much of this discussion centers on language and learning and using new languages ("borders, both visible and invisible," as one analyst has written). Though often uncomfortable, such efforts are essential in order to construct and illumine new borders and spaces, better suited for understanding other peoples.

Wikipedia refers to the possibilities of transnational companies, crime, feminism, governance, psychology, and a variety of other constructs. We can see the wide-open possibilities this conception offers in terms of identity and make-up.

In practice, transnationalism refers to increased versatility and incorporation of processes that connect and define individuals, governments, and groups of all kinds (businesses, NGOs, supranational organizations, educational groups, "emergent organizations," worker's cooperatives, community assemblies, and even criminal organizations), such that they can mobilize effectively beyond state boundaries.

Individuals, groups, institutions, and states are interacting with each other in a new global amplitude, where cultural and political characteristics are combined with evolving transnational engagements. It is also said that transnationalism is a part of the process of capitalist globalization, which indicates a darker, perhaps exploitative side of this issue, which I have rejected.

Taiwan can most assuredly see itself in all of these lights, with many transnational/transitional actors having an impact here. Probably one key actor (though not that as such) is the social movements that have rocked

Taiwan in recent years, with their efforts to redefine politics and culture. Such movements are in effect challenging the role of the state in national affairs and bringing citizens into the conversation. A look at Taiwan in these lights is truly enlightening: From the early democracy demonstrations to the Wild Lily Movement, the Wild Strawberry activists, the recent successes in LGBT rights, the Sunflower protests, and so forth, it has been a very active scene in Taiwan for many, many years. To be perfectly frank, these movements may not be "transnational" in the true sense, though to be sure many people of other nationalities have assumed roles in them, indicating a blending of borders that is very much transnational. Most importantly, this indicates a new view onto what national/world affairs actually are and can be and how such movements transgress the limits and norms of ordinary politics and (now seemingly hidebound) states. Such movements are in essence actors who are having an influence on how the state functions and makes decisions in a borderless environment. Taiwanese social movements have to be sure done all of this.

In a related action, the International Federation for Human Rights announced in May that it will hold its forum in Taipei this fall, a major development in human rights activism in Taiwan. Such a move is truly "transnational" in scope, with many countries and other organizations participating in a movement that truly does attempt to eliminate boundaries among people. And this is by no means the first such international assembly that has occurred in Taiwan. There are many conferences and meetings every year, and an event like the 2017 *Universiade* was a major accomplishment, indicating a transnational focus in the nation. These events and summits are yielding collective actions locally, nationally, and internationally, and in turn forging links across national borders amid a new global civil society. In these ways these transnational constructs are interconnected networks, with such systems promoting relationships addressing common issues, despite geographical "limitations" (we can hardly call them that any more). Such is the "shrinking" of the global space in today's world.

Some have argued that diasporas, of which there are many historical examples, are a precursor to modern transnationalism. I have written about the Taiwanese diaspora worldwide since World War II and how this has had a significant effect internationally. The migration of Taiwanese to other countries in modern times has yielded a new Taiwanese transnational identity, a mutual identity, which creates itself across borders and back again. With Taiwan having shaped the modern world in significant ways, giving so much back, I wrote in 2018, this might one day comprise an epic historicity that will match others of the past ("Taiwanese settling far and wide: a global view," February 5, 2018).

Education is probably one other key area that is having a transnational impact, and here again Taiwan is in the driver's seat. The nation is no doubt internationalizing its educational methodologies and systems dramatically, and up to 10 percent of all students in Taiwan (over 100,000) are now from other countries. I myself have experienced this just this semester, when fully eight Indonesian students attended my English conversation class at National Taiwan University of Science and Technology (the most popular Taiwan school for foreign students I have read). Such interaction is a truly wonderful thing for Taiwan.

Taiwan: A transnational state in the true sense, with all that can bring to a nation. Reciprocity, sharing, collaboration, exchange, a fluidity and communicative cloverleaf that will take Taiwan into the twenty-first century in the most rewarding and fruitful ways.

In Chap. 6, "The Future in Taiwan," I will examine arts in Taiwan in some detail, but first I turn in my following chapter, "The Taiwan Aesthetic," to an even deeper investigation of arts and aesthetics in this nation.

CHAPTER 5

The Taiwan Aesthetic

I turn now to an idea I have communicated to others in the past, the existence of a "Taiwan aesthetic," that is, a set of ideas about style, taste and expression, and a world view expressed through outward appearance, behavior, and actions. This might be called a "philosophy of ideas," a conception much too complex to be taken on completely here. But let it stand as I have conveyed it: a *Weltanschauung*, something of a cosmology, a posture from which we view the world and its visual principles (optic, discernable, sensible, and even that which is *being*, to say nothing of that which is *innovative*). This is all sounding like identity, which we have examined.

Due to the complexity of these conceptions and impressions, I may be going out on a limb here—but I like this idea in terms of Taiwan as I have seen and observed it. But the simple fact I ask myself is "do I really know and understand 'the Taiwan aesthetic' at all?" After all, growing up in the West, I was largely detached from Chinese art and its concepts, and Chinese/Asian art like ink and wash painting, jade artifacts, nationalist Chinese opera, Chinese gardens, bronze works, ceramics, and even calligraphy (which looked to me, like other Westerners, like little more than children's scribbling) were for the most part unknown to me. I was in my way an aesthetically oriented youth (a poet, a musician), and I liked beautiful art like Mozart, Picasso, Rembrandt, Michelangelo, da Vinci, Manet, and Monet; striking, intense art like *The Scream* by Edward Munch, *The Third of May 1808* by Goya, and *La Danse* by Henri Matisse;

D. Pendery, *Taiwan—A Light in the East*,
https://doi.org/10.1007/978-981-15-5604-3_5

impressionistic, modern art by van Gogh, Pissarro, Renoir, Rothko, Pollock, and Wesselmann; some alternative art such as performance art and spoken word; and this to say nothing of my passionate love for rock and other modern music. It can be seen that I was pretty much focused on the Western art world, and the very idea of Asian art was fairly foreign to me.

Taiwan in many ways bases its aesthetic ideas on Chinese art (much of it ancient), and this is understandable. Without question China, with its immense oeuvre of some of the greatest art every created, has had a huge impact on art worldwide, and the little Chinese-speaking neighbor to the east of the Middle Kingdom has been taken into this thrall. The Chinese aesthetic (if I can truly count myself as an authentic observer) may be what one observers has called a "well-integrated interdisciplinary approach, [with the] avoidance of rigid dichotomies, [a] balancing of binary opposites, and [a] firm grounding in the sociopolitical realities" (https://www.oxfordbibliographies.com). But I think much more is at work. For one thing, Chinese art and aesthetics are often abstract and esoteric to the extreme. One wonders exactly where this came from, though I think a glance at Chinese culture at large, and the Chinese people, indicates how this populace simply enjoys such complexity and elaboration. Perhaps the Chinese idiom "一絲不苟" (yīsībùgǒu)—to be meticulous, to cross one's T's—points toward this, or maybe "不可思議" (bùkěsīyì)—to be inconceivable, unbelievable. This might be called a refined Chinese craftsmanship as well as the elevation and instruction of a desire for the natural, the innate. To be sure the power of nature is common in Chinese art (often seen in ink paintings, with their seeming remoteness, distance, and overlapping and coinciding images seen in perspectival and panoramic views). We see many Chinese paintings in which image and perspective seem to be "floating," as if existent in the wind and air. Often images are poised in unrealistic proportions, and mists are used to suggest an enigmatic, insurmountable distance that is not suggested by the actual proportions.

Additionally, we might look at a cornerstone of Chinese culture, calligraphy in writing, and see some light here. Here we see "the use of an ideographic language, which requires the rote learning of thousands of characters, and the ability to reproduce these characters with technical perfection" (Jacques, 199). The quest for perfection, often seen in Chinese education and culture, could be a hint at their aesthetic.

The Chinese aesthetic, it seems, cannot be said to focus on the representational, mimetic, or figurative and instead explores variegated perspectives, narratives, and transcendence. The integration of poetry, painting, and calligraphy (called the "three perfections" in China) has long been a mark of Chinese aesthetic ideas and practice, and this is an idea I can see into, though it is in its way remote from the Western ideals I am familiar with. Viewers must make their own judgments to what extent these values are incorporated into Taiwanese art, based on a few of the following photos of artwork. But again, all of the above seems distant from my own understanding and view of what art can be and the aesthetic actually present in my own perception. I'll have to do my best to see into this crystal ball. Taiwan itself, no doubt, bases some of its approaches on these ideas, but in turn, it no doubt has an independent view onto its own art. To be sure there are many excellent artists from Taiwan, in areas of painting and sculpture, film, music, calligraphy, opera, modern art, poetry and literature, music, public art, architecture, and more.

A number of traditional arts and activities are enjoyed in Taiwan. Glove puppetry is an art form that integrates literary motifs, music, and voice acting. Oil paper umbrellas play an important role in the life of the Hakka people (a native tribe in Taiwan), and they are symbols of good fortune. Dough figures are a traditional folk art in Chinese culture, with the figures fashioned from steamed sticky rice and flour dough and called "rice sculptures." Chinese knots were once used not only to fasten objects but also to record experience. The knots have a symmetrical design and represent traditional Chinese aesthetic values. Scented sachets (pomanders) are worn during the Dragon Boat Festival in June. In the past, people ground up minerals and plants and wrapped them into small pieces of cloth to make a sachet. These were worn around the neck and released a scent that kept away insects and bacteria, which was seen as important in early medicinal uses. Tops are toys dating from ancient times and still enjoy great popularity today. Traditional kites are made of narrow bamboo strips and cotton paper. There are standard flat kites and sculptured kites in shapes of dragons, centipedes, and other whimsical figures. Diabolos are juggling props, whirled and tossed on a string connected to two sticks, one held in each hand. As the diabolo accelerates, it issues a humming sound. Experienced performers can simultaneously spin multiple diabolos and toss them high into the air. Diabolos are incorporated into dances and other performances. All of these arts and activities are important in Taiwan, but as I have noted, none are really ready to break onto the world stage. I am inclined to think about these cultures/arts as somewhat an "internal" consideration, which is to say that in some respects, nobody much cares whether these facets of aesthetics thrive externally in the world at large. It is always a *people's art*, ability, and aesthetic, individual features of a land and its citizenry (above in part from https://eng.taiwan.net.tw/m1.aspx?sNo=0002008).

All that I discuss here I again posit could be viewed in terms of Taiwanese identity, as I have examined, and I hope readers will see these data in these lights.

Of course, in the following I will not look at much of what I refer to here, and these photos are of "art," proper (painting, drawing, photography, etc.). This may be a bit limited, but that is the reality of publishing in a book. And so, with that, let us take a look at some Taiwanese art and aesthetics. Some of these photos were taken by the author, and I may not have exact locations and/or names for the works. I apologize for this and ask the reader to simply take it in and realize that it was all done and displayed in Taiwan. To be sure, in my travels across this land, I have seen countless examples of great art, both private and public (some hardly "art" at all, but simply a local decoration, building, etc.). I look forward to sharing it with you, readers. Note, of course, that other works shown below are well-known and being shown in museums in Taiwan. Below I will not look at great Chinese art, proper, with the vast collection held at the National Palace Museum in Taipei offering this rich heritage to visitors Observe figures 5-1 to 5.11 so see four famous Taiwanese art works, and photos of aesthetic designs and modes from around Taiwan by the author.

Fig. 5.1 Temple rooftop, with the usual occult, somewhat arcane design

Fig. 5.2 Elaborate temple sculpture

Fig. 5.3 A beautiful temple ceiling in Taiwan

Fig. 5.4 "Courtyard with Banana Trees," Liao Chi-chun, 1928

Fig. 5.5 Aboriginal dance

Fig. 5.6 Temple pagoda

Fig. 5.7 "Sunset at Danshui 1935," © Chen Cheng-po/Wikimedia

Fig. 5.8 Temple art

Fig. 5.9 "Still Life-Bull Head," Chen Yin-huei, 1983

Fig. 5.10 Temple roof line

Fig. 5.11 "Know It's White, Keep Silent When It's Black," Tung Yang-Tzu, 1990

CHAPTER 6

The Future in Taiwan

As I consider possible futures in Taiwan, I admit to the reader that as I sit here at my desk on an ordinary Tuesday evening, I have not framed any grand plan or strategy, some impressive tome about that which is forthcoming, to impart to humanity. As to my own future in Taiwan, I will reflect on this in the conclusion of this book. As I reflect on the future and its relation to the past and the present, I am drawn to St. Augustine, who wrote, "What about those two times, past and future: in what sense do they have real being, if the past no longer exists and the future does not exist yet? As for the present time, if that were always present and never slipped away into the past, it would not be time at all; it will be eternity." (296)

In effect, I have already covered many major issues that could impact Taiwan's future. I have looked at Taiwan's history, and the nation's history is a "passport" to its future (the term is from the October 2015 issue of *BBC History Magazine*). History in these lights is ever being written and rewritten, interpreted and reinterpreted, and no doubt always being disputed along ideological, psychological, spiritual, and cultural lines. History will always be more than looking back onto the past and is instead an engagement with the present and from there the future (Augustine just commented on this). In a word, and as I have written, historical awareness is a tart blend of the past, present, and future. I would not say anything except that Taiwan's history, checkered though it may be, and its present, volatile though *it is*, all point to a likely bright future.

D. Pendery, *Taiwan—A Light in the East*,
https://doi.org/10.1007/978-981-15-5604-3_6

But there is much more at stake here. The influence and at times hostility of China toward Taiwan are serious issues and often leave Taiwan's future an open question and even in doubt. I have looked at this possibility and also considered the likelihood of possible reunification/integration with China or the possibility of an Asian Union (I am a rare believer in this possibility and commented on this possibility above). Contrariwise, I have looked in detail at the possibility of Taiwanese independence and how this could impact not least China but the entire world. In these lights, I have looked at the possibility of peace and war in Taiwan, with all of the impact this could have on life here in the future.

In terms of my Asian Union, Dr. Damm commented that it would be difficult, because of the varying sizes, populations, and power structures evident in Asia (though the same could be said of the European Union). "If an Asian Union would include China (or even Indonesia)," said Damm, "then basically one country would be much more powerful than the rest. And an Asian Union without these countries, would not be tolerated by China and/or Indonesia. Tricky." Tricky, no doubt (that sounds like Asian politics), but I maintain my stance that it could be of great value to Asia and the world.

I have considered a number of external actors and their views onto Taiwan and how they feel about Taiwan's prospects going forward. In sum, many world leaders and most other people look at Taiwan's future in a fairly positive light.

I have looked at key current issues that will be important in Taiwan's future, including the UN debate (and/or other roles Taiwan might take on in the world); the question of neutrality; to some extent an extension of the current *status quo* on the island (a peaceful but thorny proposition); the possibility of a "collapse" in Taiwan and many other risks that beset the nation; consensus and the political conversation in the country; questions about the value and validity of Taiwan's free economy; Taiwan as a shining city on a hill, a transnational state that looks to be in the best possible position for the future; and various other contemporary political considerations.

Readers know the result of the 2020 Taiwan presidential election, and this is clearly a shining light into the future of this free, democratic country, at peace with all the other great free democracies in the world.

I have looked at happiness of Taiwanese students and a greater happiness in Taiwan at large and what this could implicate for the future. We all hope for happiness in our lives ahead, whichever nation we hail from, whether students, teachers, or any other citizen.

I am inclined to think about culture/arts and Taiwan's future. As noted above, culture and arts are always somewhat internal, hugging close to the contours of a land and its people—the interior and exterior in arts and culture, as I have looked at. Again, as I have said, I do not think the majority of local culture and arts in Taiwan are positioned to become of global prominence—and again to repeat, one may argue whether prominence is truly important in terms of the future prospects of a people and place. Yes, there is some good art, music, and filmmaking in Taiwan, but, say in terms of pop music—yes some good music is being made—such music, sung in Chinese, is not about to become a global phenomenon. Classical musicians (any language they speak does not make much difference) might be different and could be seen as globally important, but this is not generally seen as truly world-shaking in its impact (though of course there are some musicians that reach this level). Ang Lee has certainly had an impact in film around the world, and there has been some other good Taiwanese filmmaking, but, Lee aside, the genre is still not there yet. There are good painters in Taiwan, a few who have reached a fair status globally, but none that I know of who have truly broken through to the first rank. In these respects, as noted, Taiwanese culture may be making a *local impact*—but it is not ready to graduate to much greater. Nothing wrong with this, very similar to most other local cultures worldwide, which are all, in their way, evincing something great for their *native* futures. Much of what I examine here can, again, be seen in terms of Taiwanese identity.

Related to the above is the issue of tourism in Taiwan (needless to say, many tourists visit countries to experience local values, arts, and culture). It is estimated that tourism will become the largest industry in the world, with highest value add and sales of any commercial enterprise, soon. The UN World Tourism Organization reported this year that international tourist arrivals increased 6 percent to 1.4 billion in 2018, two years ahead of forecasts, and Statista reported that tourism contributed 8.27 trillion dollars to the global economy. That's economic power, but there is much more to tourism than this. "The journey not the arrival matters," said

T.S. Eliot, while *Destination Advantage* wrote, "Tourism brings people together and opens our eyes to a variety of cultures and beliefs that we may not have had a chance to experience" (https://destinationadvantage.com/the-value-of-tourism/). It is experiences like these that indicate bright future experience by way of tourism, and in these respects, Taiwan is in a good position. In a word, visitors to the country take positive views with them when they return home, which elevates Taiwan's status in the world. Taiwan is not the most visited country in Asia, but the *Taipei Times* reported in June 2019 that visitors to the country had exceeded one million for the first time, up 24.72 percent from 2018. Taiwan has seen such growth in tourism for many years. Interestingly, Taiwan is seen as a leader in medical tourism (with 414,000 visits most recently [*Taipei Times*, May 06, 2019]) and also in the potential for "rainbow" LGBT tourism after Taiwan became the first Asian country to legalize gay marriage.

Related to the above, I am inclined to think that Taiwan's business community and industry, with its famed electronics and precision manufacturing industries and a few other global businesses (Giant Bikes, Cathay Life Insurance, Taiwan Cement, SPR Coffee, 85° Coffee and Bakery), points toward good days ahead. The days of the Taiwan Miracle may be over, but economic growth in Taiwan has been steady and strong, and though I have criticized this view above, I have also noted that this does bring contentment to people. In another related area, I view Taiwan space technology as developing positively in the future. The National Space Organization has overseen the FORMOSAT satellite program, which has launched communications satellites, as well as those performing ionospheric research, earth surface mapping, GPS occultation studies of the upper atmosphere, magnetic field research, and meteorological studies. An exhibition was held in Taipei in 2019 recognizing 40 years of cooperation with the United States in space exploration and astronomy (Fig. 6.1).

Additionally, urban and local development in Taiwan points toward a bright future. Taiwan's cities are developing rapidly, and many advances are leading the way—new transportation, housing, architectural refurbishment and infrastructure expansion, public services, health care (long a high point in Taiwan), educational improvement (which I have looked at), technological advances (many Taiwan cities might be called "smart"), and cultural spectacles. I have often been amazed not least at Taipei's planning and development, to say nothing of the brilliant culture and arts displays and exhibitions here. Few cities in Taiwan are far behind, and what was

Fig. 6.1 Taiwan Semiconductor Manufacturing Company

once a fairly mundane or worse, dilapidated nation is now a bright innovator in all of these areas (I read once that in 1960 you could still see horses, cattle, and rickshaws on Taipei's streets; to be sure that is no longer true). The countryside can be seen in these lights, and improvements to the environment and landscapes in Taiwan are also proceeding apace. But we must not forget that over four billion people worldwide—more than half the global population—live in metropolises. This trend is expected to continue, and by 2050, the urban population will more than double, and nearly 7 of 10 people in the world will live in cities (the World Bank). To be sure Taiwan is a city-lover's paradise, and municipalities north to south are advancing rapidly.

I have covered most of these issues in the works above, and they point in various ways toward Taiwan's future(s), both positive and negative. What more is there to say? That is a very difficult question—predicting the future is usually seen as the demesne of fools and quacks. In sum, readers can see that in any event I have a very positive outlook on Taiwan, and I could probably end this discussion right here. There are a handful of observers and commentators in Taiwan who complain about economic growth and other political concerns here, and there is always the antagonistic anti-China group, a very influential assembly in Taiwan. These people are negative to the extreme and refuse to look at possible positive outcomes. This is a whole lot less than worldly, let alone generous. There is little or no future in views like these.

In terms of what I say here, however, admittedly conflict with China is a major concern, and this reality does not look to be greatly diminishing at this time. But I think that Taiwan as a democratic example could yet have influence in China and, more importantly, that the Chinese people do not in fact greatly desire conflict and war with Taiwan. Here again I take an essentially positive and constructive view. The heated desire for struggle and even war is mainly the domain of the hotheads and militarists, who do have a substantial impact (in both China and Taiwan), but this cannot change the will of the people. Chinese people in sum view Taiwanese people as part of their lives and to some extent culture (maybe not one "family" as Taipei Mayor Ko Wen-je has said, but close enough; family relations are not always 100 percent amicable). The two nations are unique in definite ways, apart in many respects, but in the main they are one people who for the most part love one another. Again, there are a number of commentators who would in effect denounce what I say here, but I stand by my views.

To be sure there are some serious problems and drawbacks to the life and politics that Chinese people have crafted, and the differences with Taiwan are pronounced. I have mentioned their president, Xi Jinping, and to be sure he has been much less than accommodating to Taiwan. Readers are aware of these differences that separate an authoritarian, socialist, and/or communist state from a free democracy and economy. Professor Damm comments that "it was 1989 when it became clear that Taiwan was an open society, and China had issues. China was developing infrastructure, there was poverty reduction, which is still true, but I'm not satisfied with the situation." To make matters worse, it appears that Xi has installed himself as "president for life," and this may not change for some time (and is to be sure a decided difference from Taiwan). But then again it could change (and *will change* sooner or later), and who knows what that future holds? A more obliging Chinese president in terms of Taiwan? It could be possible (long shot though it appears to be at this time). In sum, politics are fluid, ever-changing, and the political differences between Taiwan and China are not permanent, and better outcomes could be achieved in the future—let's hope.

With the above said, an important future consideration in Taiwan that I have not brought up is environmental concerns—which was briefly examined above in "Taiwan threatened by myriad risks." As noted in that work, the looming environmental threat could cause internal unrest and conflict, as well as criticism and censure from abroad, to say nothing of a lot of discomfort for citizens of Taiwan—to be sure not promising signals in Taiwan's future. Professor Damm brought this up briefly and observed that "in Hamburg and Marseille (or the lakes in Berlin) I can go the city beach and dive into the water. Not in Taiwan. Sigh."

Let me turn now to one final examination of politics and their influence in Taiwan. In recent months, an action has been taking place that I initially tended to discount as seriously impacting Taiwanese life and politics. Here I refer to the recent protests in Hong Kong, which have garnered worldwide attention. I should say that I have written no commentary on these events, and thus I have published nothing about them. Let this commentary be my first.

If I say that I tended to discount these events, then I here also say that I think I was no doubt wrong. I now see that the months-long pro-democracy, and in essence anti-government, demonstrations in Hong Kong have in fact had a significant impact in Taiwan. We will see this often in the following (Fig. 6.2).

Let's take a look at recent developments in Hong Kong and their impact on Taiwan's future. Unrest essentially began in Hong Kong in 2014, with the Umbrella Movement, which sought greater freedom and independence from China. The name arose from the use of umbrellas as a tool for passive resistance to the Hong Kong Police's use of pepper spray to disperse the crowd during an occupation of the city demanding more transparent elections, which was sparked by the decision of the Standing Committee of the National People's Congress approving a selective pre-screening of candidates for the 2017 election of Hong Kong's chief executive (*Wikipedia*, "Umbrella Movement"). This was in essence a non-violent protest, and the response of the police was often criticized as overbearing and even oppressive. Interestingly enough, it was shortly before this movement that the Sunflower Student Movement erupted in Taiwan, which

Fig. 6.2 Hong Kong protests

protested the passing of the Cross-Strait Service Trade Agreement, an economic cooperation agreement with China, which the protesters accused Ma Ying-jeou and his government of forcing through without adequate appraisal and debate. This movement developed into an essential anti-KMT government movement and also a protest demanding greater freedom and rights in Taiwan (Fig. 6.3). To return to Hong Kong, the Umbrella Movement was really the start of the current protests, which initially sought annulment of an extradition bill in China, which would have required those arrested in Hong Kong to be tried in China proper, and then expanded into pro-democracy protests and anger against the Hong Kong Chief Executive Carrie Lam and the demand for her to step down. This is a quick look at the 2019 protests in Hong Kong.

To return to Taiwan's response to these protests, President Tsai Ing-Wen has expressed solidarity with the Hong Kong protesters. She

Fig. 6.3 Taiwan Sunflower Movement supporters in Los Angeles

announced that the ROC government would provide assistance to Hong Kong protesters who have declared they would relocate to Taiwan (which many have said they would do). The office of the president issued an announcement that said "We solemnly urge the Beijing authorities to honor their commitment to allow Hong Kong a high degree of autonomy, and not use the concern for the people of Hong Kong by Taiwan and other countries as an excuse for accusations of interference by outside forces. We also urge the Hong Kong government to avoid excessive use of force, and actively engage in dialogue to resolve its differences with the public so that conflicts can be resolved peacefully and rationally" (https://english.president.gov.tw/News/5835). In these lights, it has been noted that "Taiwan is proving [to be] an increasingly popular destination for those seeking a more open…place to live" (*Nikkei Asian Review*, October 14, 2019). *Quartz* on July 19, 2019, reported that "Taiwan is the new home for Hong Kongers seeking political safety." In terms of Taiwan's response, the *Kyodo News* reported on September 29, 2019, that tens of thousands of Taiwanese took to the streets of Taipei and major Taiwanese cities that day as part of a global "anti-totalitarianism rally" in support of Hong Kong protesters. And so, we see the impact this is having here in Taiwan (the Hong Kong protests were on the front page of the *Taipei Times* virtually every day in August, September, and October of 2019).

Taiwan's Foreign Minister Joseph Wu has called for "genuine" democratic elections to be held in Hong Kong (*The Straits Times*, July 23, 2019). Hong Kong "serves as another warning of China's constant desire to interfere and suppress democracy" Wu said (*The Times' Thunderer*, June 11, 2019). We will see more of these ideas just below.

It is felt that an exodus from Hong Kong could benefit Taiwan's economy. "If (Hong Kong) companies are looking for a new regional base which offers them the same rights and freedoms that they had in Hong Kong, Taiwan is a great choice" said the *Taiwan News* on August 24, 2019. The number of visas issued to Hong Kongers in Taiwan in June and July 2019 was 38 percent higher, at 884, than in the same period a year ago, according to the Ministry of the Interior's National Immigration Agency (*Reuters*, September 12, 2019).

As noted above Taiwan citizens have spoken up in favor of the Hong Kong protests, and in turn students in Taiwan universities have taken the protests to heart and have stood up and launched their own protests. During demonstrations here, a number of visiting Chinese students were accused of vandalizing "Lennon Walls" that supported Hong Kong. President Tsai Ing-wen ordered government agencies to impose restrictions on visitors who damaged displays or attacked Hong Kong supporters. "Chinese students damaged Lennon walls on some campuses and claimed to exercise 'democratic protests'," said Bi-yu Chang, deputy director of the Centre of Taiwan Studies at SOAS, University of London. "However, what is democracy?" she asked. "These Chinese students seemed to form a different idea about what democracy is, how it operates and the rights and responsibilities it entails. What they saw and then practiced in Taiwan are superficial 'democratic acts.' To me, their actions indicate a collective identity anxiety and a distorted vision of democracy" (*Times Higher Education*, October 25, 2019). Ah yes, the differences between China, Taiwan, and the free world….

One commentator in the *Taipei Times*, Joseph Tse-hei Lee, a Taiwanese professor in the United States, claimed on December 8 that Hong Kong was experiencing a "clash of civilizations," based on Professor Samuel P. Huntington's now infamous thesis in which he argued that conflict in the future would no longer be based on political systems and inclinations, but on clashes between cultures and "civilizations" in the world, including Latin American, Buddhist, Chinese, Hindu, Japanese, African, Orthodox (Russia and satellite states), Muslim, and Western. Lee argued that the Hong Kong "clash" pitted "liberalism and authoritarianism, and between popular demand for openness and autocratic obsession with control." Certainly, the conflict in Hong Kong is that, but the claim that it is a "civilizational clash" is ludicrous. In a letter published in the *Taipei Times* on December 9, I refuted this claim, pointing out that it is instead a political clash, a clash between governmental/administrative systems and beliefs—which are categorically not civilizations. Jacques has written that "China embodies and allows a plurality of systems, as exemplified by Hong Kong, that is alien to the nation-state" (201). Though admittedly the nation-state and the civilization are very different, we can in any event see that the notion of "plurality" does point to what I argue: a clash of authority and managerial methods.

Meanwhile US vice president Mike Pence in October 2019 delivered a hawkish speech on China, criticizing the nation's human rights record, while praising Hong Kong's pro-democracy struggles—comments that were celebrated in Taiwan. China has in turn faced up to some of these problems, saying in a communist congress that it is "facing a complicated situation of significantly increased risks and challenges domestically and abroad" (*Taipei Times*, November 1, 2019).

With all of this attention, it has dawned on me that the 2019 Hong Kong protests are indeed important in Taiwan. At one bottom line, Taiwan looks at the protesters in Hong Kong and celebrates the protester's quest for freedom and democracy, a quest that needless to say Taiwan has had a long and arduous road toward. Further, Taiwan looks at China's response to the protests, in which the country has said its "one country, two systems" model (looked at above) can be made to work, and Taiwan has almost universally rejected this. To be sure President Tsai Ing-wen, as noted, has decisively rejected this model.

When I initially saw these protests unfolding, I had a somewhat different view—a view that will not be popular in Taiwan. Here is some more background, from *Wikipedia*, "Hong Kong Basic Law." The Basic Law of the Hong Kong Special Administrative Region of the People's Republic of

China (it is important to note that Hong Kong is a Special Administrative Region, with a measure of autonomy) is a national law of the People's Republic of China (which means that citizens of Hong Kong, while nominally autonomous, are citizens of the People's Republic of China). The Basic Law was adopted on April 4, 1990, and signed by Yang Shangkun, 杨尚昆, president of the People's Republic of China from 1988 to 1993. The above makes clear that the Hong Kong Special Administrative Region is part of the People's Republic of China (though it said that Hong Kong's governing and economic systems are "separate from those of mainland China," I do not believe this is entirely true). No doubt it is true that the region has a substantial degree of autonomy and enjoys executive, legislative, economic, and independent judicial power (China had little choice but to agree to this with the handover of power from the United Kingdom in 1997), but it remains just this—a given governing body, within the People's Republic of China. In terms of economics and governance, it has been said that with the enactment of the Basic Law "the [Chinese] socialist system and policies shall *not* be practised in the Hong Kong Special Administrative Region" and that the capitalist system developed under British rule would remain unchanged for 50 years (*Wikipedia*, "Hong Kong Basic Law," emphasis added). One of the complaints of the current protests is that this has not held true. I find it hard to believe that China would not expect and enforce "socialism with Chinese characteristics" in this special administrative region, whatever autonomy it might be granted; in any case Hong Kong remains one of the most prominent capitalist market centers in the world to this day. To return to the above discussion of the extradition bill, in these lights I viewed Hong Kongers as Chinese citizens, and therefore, why should they complain if they are accused of a crime and must in turn be tried in a Chinese court? Hong Kong may have a degree of autonomy, but it is still a Chinese "region" (or territory)—which says just that: it is a place in which Chinese citizens live. In a word, "there is no scenario under which [Hong Kong] could lead a separate existence, however you define it, from the mainland," as reported in the *South China Morning Post* on August 20, 2019. Now I am not going to make many friends in Taiwan saying all of this, and even further (I am going out on a limb here), I have questioned whether today's Hong Kongers should be demanding complete freedom and in essence independence. This would be like the state of Nebraska attempting to gain independence from the United States, which could never happen (it's against the law). In fact, the United States has a similar system of self-government within its borders, in terms of the Native American Reservations (Indian Reservations, in the outdated terminology). This system is called "tribal sovereignty," a conception of the inherent authority of Native Americans (the tribes) to govern themselves, the auspices of which are referred to as "domestic dependent nations" by the US government. Associate Justice of the Supreme Court Joseph Story (1779–1845) wrote in his *Commentaries on the Constitution of the United States* that "Indians, also, in several, and probably in most, of the states…[exercise] general sovereignty and powers of government within the boundaries of the states" (439). American Indians on their home reservations have autonomy, systems of government, law enforcement bodies, and structures of law and courts that are in the main independent of US control. This system may indeed look similar to China's Special Administrative Region, but I am not aware of any Native American Reservation that has ever sought secession from the United States. As with Nebraska, that would be against the law and could never happen. And indeed, like China, the United States could and would send in its military were this ever attempted. Now there is something for the independence advocates to consider!

What is happening in Hong Kong is no doubt different from much of anything that has happened in China during its vast history (though admittedly the 1989 Tiananmen Square protests were similar, with their focus on democracy in China). China is a country with a very different history, ethics, and standards than that we see in Western states, which have to date controlled just what it means to be a "state" in the world system. In the view of Martin Jacques, China is a "civilization-state," in which the country's history, relationships, values, and prior ideals (in the main, Confucian) continue to influence the modern people and state and its distinctive political philosophy. In this way, "Politics has always been seen as coterminous with government, with little involvement from other elites or the people" (207). Jacques calls this general view "impoverished," which it might seem to Western observers, but it is key to understanding Chinese politics. In this light, I refer to the recent actions in Hong Kong. Hong Kong in the past largely approved of the Chinese government and its developments, but that has clearly changed. Rather than the past "top-down rather than bottom-up" contact with the people (Jacqueus, 207), today's Hong Kongers are demanding something new. "The state has consistently been seen as the apogee of society" in China's history (Jacques,

207), and Hong Kong no longer desires this and is seeking a true democratic outlet, freedom, continuing human rights, and the rule of law—Western concepts that have not been widely adopted in China during its many millennia. In China, the "state" (which it is not quite, according to Jacques) has long enjoyed "sovereignty over all else" (Jacques, 207). To repeat, Hong Kong is seeking to change this. They are in effect seeking to change long-held beliefs in Chinese politics, and this is going to be a challenge. A challenge that not a few people around the world hope is successful, but just this, nonetheless. Hong Kongers obviously do not like things completely as they are in China today, but in sum "the idea that different sources of authority could and should coexist was seen as ethically wrong" (Jacques, 208), and "The only accepted interest was the universal interest represented by a government" (Jacques, 208). The people and various groups in China, though they have exercised some power and a given sovereignty, in the past largely saw themselves as "a bulwark of government rather than as an autonomous interest seeking separate representation" (Jacques, 208), and thus "it is hardly surprising that China has failed to develop a civil society" (Jacques, 208). This does not sound very good to Western ears, but it is the reality in China. These ideas carry on to this day, and thus for many Chinese, Hong Kong and its recent protests are seen as an anomaly, a group that cannot rightfully make the demands they are making. Yes, Hong Kong has the right to demand change (in my view), but the Chinese people have never invited this in their provinces and spheres of influence.

With the above, in essence Hong Kong does not truly have the right to fully separate from China (Jacques also points out an overriding focus in Chinese politics is unity, and thus a separate Hong Kong would not be accepted; though this might be a possibility, it is I feel somewhat unlikely). Let me say that I am in no way against Hong Kongers demonstrating for more freedom and democracy. I have been clear in my criticism of China as an authoritarian dictatorship, and the Communist Party as a restrictive and very un-free political party. I have been a defender of freedom, rule of law, and human rights 100 percent down the line, and that can be seen in all of the work in this book. And indeed, whatever I say about Hong Kong here, after the 2020 Taiwan presidential election, it was recognized that the Hong Kong protests had had a favorable impact on the election of Tsai Ing-wen. "Hong Kong protests seen as a key factor in KMT's defeat" wrote the *Taipei Times*, with KMT Nantou chapter director Yang Li-chuan

(楊麗川) commenting that "the DPP injected a sense of urgency regarding the nation's sovereignty into the campaign through its response to the Hong Kong protests" (January 12, 2020). And indeed, my wife said after the election, "the Hong Kong protests came at just the right time for Tsai Ing-wen" (and her sister voted for a DPP candidate for the first time in her life).

In a view possibly similar to mine, Jinshan Hong and Iain Marlow wrote in the *Taipei Times* on December 20, 2019, how neighboring Macau, unlike Hong Kong, "values the riches of China above democracy." Macau has a similar territorial status as Hong Kong, but does not suffer from the high housing costs and influx of mainlanders that Hong Kong has, and the territory "benefits from the motherland a lot. We residents know this well," said Simon Sio, chairman of real-estate and investment firm Lek Hang Group. Xi Jinping visited the territory in December 2019 and praised Macau's "earnest implementation of the 'one country, two systems' framework." Unrest in Macau has been rare, and "While Hong Kong people can be mobilized by fighting for abstract value as democracy and freedom, Macau is 'interest-oriented,'" said Ieong Meng U (楊鳴宇), an assistant professor at the University of Macau's Department of Government and Public Administration. "Only very few government policies can trigger widespread social grievances."

In light of the above and previous comments, we can see that there are significant differences separating Hong Kong from Mainland China. One of the most important distinctions may be language. The majority of residents in Hong Kong most likely speak Cantonese (廣東話, guǎngdōng huà) at home, a very different language from standard Mandarin (國語 (guóyǔ, the national language, 普通話pǔtōnghuà, the common language). Cantonese is viewed as a "vital and inseparable part of the cultural identity" of Hong Kongers (*Wikipedia*, "Cantonese"), and to be sure that differentiates them from much of the rest of China. Of course, Hong Kongers can also speak Mandarin, but most likely in their everyday relationships they are speaking Cantonese. This too reminds me of the United States, where upward of 41 million people speak Spanish at home—and to be sure they are of a different ethos than most of the rest of the United States. In this respect, yes, Hong Kong is very different from most of Mainland China, and we are seeing some of these variances come to the fore in these protests.

That may be enough about Hong Kong for now (yes, I seem to have written my commentary and statement after all). I know that many people will object, some strongly, to the above analysis of the Hong Kong situation. I understand this and can see that I have in large part gone against the grain of common feeling about the protests. To be sure the majority of citizens in Taiwan at this time are strongly pro-Hong Kong and in essence anti-China. I agree with the "pro," but have never leaned toward the "anti" in these areas. This can be seen in the above argument—troublesome though it may be in some respects. Some will claim here that I am an anti-democrat and anti-human rights zealot. I think that readers of this book can see that this is absurd, and I am squarely in the corner of believers in these universal rights and privileges.

I will have to live with any criticism that is lodged against me. I speak my mind on international issues, I always have, and I will not retreat from my views. I remember the conflicts that erupted in my courses in the International Relations program at San Francisco State University as an undergraduate, not a few skirmishes that emerged from my strong views on US and international politics. The truth is, however, that the above analysis does not truly square with how I myself feel about Hong Kong. As I have stated, I believe that Hong Kongers have all rights to demand greater freedoms, voting rights, and self-determination in their city. The Native Americans are again relevant here. They have a given autonomy within US borders and quite a lot of freedom within their own borders. I have been told that Native Americans have substantial power in deciding who can live and work on their lands, and in general ordinary Americans cannot freely do these things there. But this does not change the fact that Native Americans are American citizens and must abide by US law, customs, duties, and expectations. Again, I say the same is true for Hong Kongers—within the People's Republic of China state, with its own rights, privileges, and so on. Where this is leading may be an open question at this time. I have already stated that Hong Kong obtaining a given independence is possible, and I wish them luck in their endeavors. My sincere hope is that peace and order will be maintained.

I think much of what I think and convey here may indeed have an impact on Taiwan's future. With that, let us turn to my final views on Taiwan.

We are brought back to square one: Where exactly does Taiwan stand, and what does this suggest about its future? I need not say it again (but must): Taiwan—as a free democracy, with citizen rule, individual (majority and minority) rights and privileges, free and fair elections, the rule of law, and true cooperation and compromise across all levels of society—is in a position to reap the greatest benefits for its people in the future. Conflict will happen, internally and externally, but that will not change what the people will secure and the uninhibited lives they will be able to live. Long live such freedom! This is a message that even (and especially) citizens living under authoritarian or dictatorial regimes desire to hear.

CHAPTER 7

The Termite and Taiwan

All I have examined in this work points to two views onto Taiwan, including that (1) the nation is an important international agent and independent entity, a dignified presence in global matters, and a distinguished eminence in international proceedings and transactions; but an alternative view is that (2) Taiwan is a non-entity, a wholly non-independent and in effect powerless international operative—not a "nation" at all, little more than an onlooker, one which can be all but ignored in world affairs. I need hardly inform readers that this has been an important issue in international relations for many years, pitting two very different views of just what Taiwan is and means, and in turn giving rise to many polarized and often fierce opinions in the argument. Readers of this book can clearly see which side of the dispute I am on—a fierce defender of the universal aims of pluralist democracy, citizen interests and privileges, human rights, egalitarianism, and emancipations. This view is in opposition to the world of authoritarian dictatorship, autocracy, absolutism, and despotism, wherever they may be lurking in the world.

But again, this all suggests more, which is to say—exactly what place, part, and position do Taiwan actually have in all of this? After all, with its shady and often murderous authoritarian past, Taiwan can hardly claim to be fully above the darkness I have described (such as we can say, for it is clear that in fact many inhabitants in Taiwan never embraced this world view). This all makes me ponder, just what kind of state is Taiwan? Free, democratic, embracing universal principles of liberty and justice? Clearly

D. Pendery, *Taiwan—A Light in the East*,
https://doi.org/10.1007/978-981-15-5604-3_7

yes nowadays in most ways, but still we ask, just what role are you playing on the world stage now, Taiwan? Participant or bystander? There are many people who may appreciate and celebrate what you are doing, but at the same time others dismiss you as not worth the time of day, a very, very insignificant actor. By no means an autocracy any more, but still a feeble presence in international affairs, haunted by a tortured past, a nation that features a Lincoln-esque statue of a tyrant who has little or no place or entitlement in today's world.

With the above, I am inclined to think of Taiwan as a somewhat unusual *haut-parleur* at the world rostrum today. This is to say that Taiwan has a dual role and is simultaneously forceful and flaccid, burgeoning and back-sliding, in its interactions and impact in the world. Taiwan may in this sense be something of a termite gnawing at the foundations of global existence and incident, at once strong and weak. I don't really like referring to Taiwan as a humble insect this way, but it seems to me to be an apt metaphor for just what Taiwan is—that is, as noted, an entity both strong and weak, evincing potent change but also living an existence threatened by everything around it. This idea has been touched on by others, with David A. Baldwin saying that within a given "multidimensional characteristic of power" in global affairs today, one can see nations both "simultaneously strong and weak-e.g. powerful with respect to some scopes of some actors and weak with respect to other scopes of other actors" (497).

I think this may apply to Taiwan. As Baldwin writes that a nation can be powerful in the aspects he notes, I see Taiwan as "powerful" in comparison to a number of other nations, even ultra-powerful nations like China, Germany, the United Kingdom, Japan, and the United States. Taiwan's citizen democracy referendums, for example, may be "revolutionizing democracy" according to the *Washington Post* (October 5, 2018), and Taiwan's public vote (as opposed to the US electoral college) is "completely transparent, low tech, open and inspires confidence," according to Kharis Templeman, a research scholar at Stanford University. Such elements of Taiwan's democracy are having a global impact.

Other important points about power include Taiwan's extremely well-functioning national health system (a pride of the nation, and this includes an excellent life expectancy); infrastructure and transportation development; incredible strengths in technology, biotech, pharmaceuticals, software,. and industries at large; a flawed but in general first-rate education system; a vibrant civil society; highly competitive export corporations and high foreign exchange reserves; and what, in spite of their limitations, can be seen as excellent relations with most other countries in the world. All of this says a lot about the strengths that uphold Taiwan's indeed sturdy position in the world today.

T. V. Paul goes on that a "strong-weak state" "is strong…in its legitimacy and control over most parts of the country," but it is "weak in terms of its ability to provide welfare and internal security" (7). Paul refers here principally to India, which I don't think I can compare Taiwan to, but I will continue with this basic idea in looking at Taiwan.

And so, what exactly do I mean? Importantly, though Taiwan may be strong in its validity and authority over the country—Taiwan's government is certainly a valid and responsible leader in these respects, and its military is seen as a powerful force providing protection for its citizens. The nation's press, however, though free in all aspects, is often seen as a relatively careless and cavalier actor in national and international affairs. And in turn Taiwan politicians themselves are sometimes viewed as similarly high-handed, seen hurling chairs at one another rather than participating in governance, proper. On the other hand, Taiwan is anything but weak in its ability to provide welfare for its citizens. Economically, Taiwan's world leadership need hardly be noted, and its people are comfortable in a well-functioning and mostly advancing economy. Taiwan is highly developed, ranked 7th economically in Asia and 22nd in the world by purchasing power parity (Wikipedia, "International Rankings of Taiwan"); it is included in the International Monetary Fund's advanced economies group and is seen as a high-income economy by the World Bank (Wikipedia, "Economy of Taiwan"). Many nations have followed in the footsteps of Taiwan's export-led, technology-powered, immigrant-friendly, small-and-medium enterprise-focused, and very infrastructure developed economy. Add to this Taiwan's commitment to education, an advanced system as noted with tens of thousands of foreigners who have come to participate. Its national health system is seen as a world leader—"Health care in Taiwan remains one of the best in the world for your money, according to Bloomberg's annual ranking of health care efficiency" (*The News Lens*, September 21, 2018). Taiwan's provision of external security was noted above, and in terms of internal security, Taiwan was ranked by the Institute of Economics and Peace's annual Global Peace Index the sixth safest country in the Asia Pacific and 34th safest globally (*Taiwan News*, June 7, 2018).

In what might seem obvious, I have already discussed Taiwan's major weakness in the world, in that the country is not the independent nation it claims to be. I stand by this analysis and am firmly convinced it is strongly based on international norms and law. This puts Taiwan well behind other states with limited recognition, including the likes of the State of Palestine, with non-member observer state status in the UN—well above Taiwan's straightforward non-membership—and with official recognition of 138 of the 193 UN member states. Other states are also non-members, but at least have some recognition by other UN members—the Republic of Kosovo and the Sahrawi Arab Democratic Republic are recognized by 98 and 32 UN members, respectively, far more than the 15 that recognize the Republic of China. The names of these states would hardly be recognized by many people worldwide, which at least Taiwan can claim to (though it is often mistaken for Thailand).

This lack of recognition by other states and the UN is obviously Taiwan's greatest weakness—though a few people claim that such lack of recognition does not detract from Taiwan's status as such. To be sure, as noted, Taiwan (less than the Republic of China) is "recognized" by most people worldwide and is viewed as a "state," as such. And "even if all 15 diplomatic partners leave, the substantive impact on Taiwan may be small," wrote the *Taiwan News* on October 18, 2019. Taiwan "will continue to maintain international relevance with or without formal diplomatic recognition," the article continues, but this "requires creative actions by Taiwan to deepen unofficial relations with non-recognizing states like the United States and Australia and to enhance person-to-person diplomatic efforts." Taiwan has proven adept at exactly these measures, to say nothing of many other "strengths" that Taiwan has, as examined above and throughout this work, the majority of which are seen in light of state-like status.

But to return to that which is weak in Taiwan, some that are mentioned include foreign trade that is vulnerable to conditions and/or manipulation by China and the United States; massive relocation of labor and expertise (much to China, and indeed a "brain drain" has been observed in Taiwan in recent years); weakening industrial development and associated employment (and again, China is blamed for much of this); lack of competitiveness in the service sector (this may be a reflection of most such industries speaking primarily Chinese); and, to repeat, Taiwan's growing isolation on the international diplomatic scene—which of course includes a weak position *vis-à-vis* China, which is not something any country wants in the world today (the Tsai administration's anti-China stance and actions here are a problem and a drawback).

Thinking about all of the above, let me return to my metaphor of the termite. Termites might be relatively weak on the surface—a little bug that can be squashed underfoot and which in turn in its native environment does have a number of enemies and predators—any fox, galago, numbat, mouse, or pangolin that can bore into a termite mound/nest can veritably wipe out a colony, and even tiny ants can do much damage. Some might view Taiwan as little more than this on the world stage, a little creature that can be, and often is, squashed by larger competitors. The termite, however, is an insect that can virtually bring down a house, and often they do. "The damage caused by termites costs the southwestern United States approximately $1.5 billion each year in wood structure damage, but the true cost of damage worldwide cannot be determined," says Wikipedia ("Termites"). Anyone who has experienced termite damage can affirm this, and it shows how a seemingly weak little insect can in fact have a significant impact. The same could be said for Taiwan, as this little player in the world has had an outsized influence, as we have seen in much of the above. No doubt countries worldwide would agree, and a quick glance at what has been said about Taiwan by major actors confirms this—and we have looked at many of these statements in this book. Taiwan is not quite the "little country" commonly perceived—it is the 57th largest in the world according to Worldometer (about the size of Australia, no "small country").

Termites are "among the most successful groups of insects on Earth, colonizing most landmasses except Antarctica" (Wikipedia, "Termites"). Taiwan may not have quite this expanse, but it is making an impact around the world. Taiwan, the little country that could—bringing down the house. Not a few people believe Taiwan has done something like this economically and will do something in this way politically with mainland China in the not-too-distant future—by way of the nation's vibrant and competitive democratic polity—with "society's mobilization and growing assertiveness" limiting the power of the state Leviathan (Acemoglu and Robinson, 323), and in turn indicating how the nation has taken the reins of citizen power and vindication. Taiwan was given a score of 93 out of 100 by Freedom in the World 2019, more than underscoring the state's potential power in these areas. "Taiwan proves that a determined nation can attain democracy, freedom and prosperity peacefully," wrote Rigger in 2011. Xi Jinping remarked on November 3, 2020, that "China's people's democracy is a type of whole-process democracy," but few observers feel that China is very close to true democracy (diplomat.com, December 6,

2019). Taiwan has "demonstrated the idea that liberal democracy provides a strong foundation for challenging China's interests," which may have positive implications, but must not be seen as an overt "trial" of the Chinese way of life, or some sort of accusation of wrongdoing (ibid.).

This all says so much. Yes, Taiwan's diplomatic problems point in another direction, but the potential lack of actual impact here has been considered—and the potential for truly great impact is in the air. This may be enough on this short theoretical aside, and I hope it points to yet more that is positive about this little island nation that could. With that, I turn to comments on the COVID-19 pandemic, and its impact in Taiwan and the world.

CHAPTER 8

COVID-19: Taiwan and the World

The COVID-19 coronavirus outbreak took the world by storm from January to May 2020, and it went further after that, and the fear in the air was no different in Taiwan—but fortunately the situation on the ground here was better than average. Though the virus posed a looming threat, and commentators were saying that there was no end in sight, the Taiwan government was recognized internationally for its effective handling of the crisis and keeping the infected to a minimum. The island was commended for its actions during the pandemic. According to Wikipedia:

> The Taiwanese government integrated data from the national healthcare system, immigration, and customs authorities to aid in the identification and response to the virus. Government efforts are coordinated through the National Health Command Center (NHCC) of the Taiwan Centers for Disease Control (headed by Minister of Health and Welfare Chen Shih-chung [陳時中]).
>
> The Journal of the American Medical Association states that Taiwan engaged in 124 discrete action items to prevent the spread of the disease, including early screening of flights from Mainland China and the tracking of individual cases.
>
> Taiwan's handling of the outbreak has received international praise for its effectiveness in quarantining the people and by using the "electronic fence" to slow down the virus, despite being unable to gather WHO information due to being barred by China, and is seen as the model for other countries to learn from. As of 29 March, 29,915 tests had been conducted in Taiwan with the vast majority not confirming a coronavirus diagnosis.

D. Pendery, *Taiwan—A Light in the East*,
https://doi.org/10.1007/978-981-15-5604-3_8

> Starting 19 March foreign nationals were barred from entering Taiwan, with some exceptions, such as those carrying out the term of a business contract, holding valid Alien Resident Certificates, diplomatic credentials, or other official documentation and special permits. ("2020 coronavirus pandemic in Taiwan")

That said, there was still threat in the air, and as the cases in Taiwan rose to over 500 by the end of August, I was more than extremely worried. I and my family were involved in this, and all the necessary actions that were required were taken. Wearing face masks outdoors and cleaning of the hands with alcohol solution became a necessity at all times. My work in

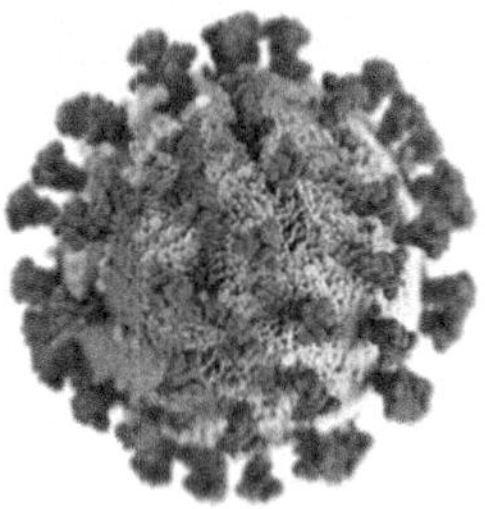

classrooms was somewhat intimidating, and oddly enough I noted a number of students did not wear face masks. Shame on them. I heard tell of one student, spotted without a mask, reported to the school, and when he was investigated it was found that his brother had recently returned from a European hot spot. That spelled suspension for him. To be sure, travelers returning to Taiwan, both Taiwanese and foreigners who live here, were soon recognized as "importers" of the virus. Many Taiwanese students returned home from the United States, Australia, and Europe, justly believing that the situation was safer here, but actually bringing the virus with them when they arrived. They were promptly put under a two-week quarantine when this was found, an excellent effort by the government.

Cleaning of our apartment and of course our bodies became a daily ritual (I mopped outside of our home, and inside, with bleach solutions). Visits to clinics or the hospital were rather fearful, and my wife was strict in her control of cleansing ourselves and disposal of face masks after such visits. I was instructed to avoid all contact with others, and even when I played tennis with a foreign contact, I wore my face mask when we spoke.

I watched the international situation with true anxiety, not least the United States as it became the most infected area on the planet, with 6,929,395 cases and 200,000 deaths as I completed the proofs of this book in early September. I had thought the United States would be relatively safe, but it spread amazingly fast there. I gave credit to President Donald Trump when he announced a national emergency after his initial careless comments and actions (he was later criticized for many facets of his response). And of course, the global impact was far more serious. Everyone was aware of the desperate situations in the United States, Brazil, Italy, Iran, Korea, and China. By this time, it was truly a pandemic, and deaths in the millions were seen as very possible, which would place the coronavirus in the class of the worst epidemics of the past. Very, very scary.

I can only say that I was happy to be in Taiwan during all of this. The government response was amazingly effective, and essentially the disease was fully controlled and not spreading among the population. There was no lockdown or huge closures of businesses and schools, all the way into September, as I completed proofs. While businesses and institutions were closing down worldwide, this had not happened in Taiwan (I read one editorial in the *Taipei Times* that did recommend that President Tsai Ing-wen declare an emergency, and I could see it happening).

During the crisis the WHO came under severe criticism for its blocking of Taiwan from any role. WHO Director-General Tedros Adhanom Ghebreyesus was chastised for kowtowing to China, and indeed it seemed that he was always giving great credit to the country for controlling the virus, which in reality seemed far from the truth. China's claims that it was in no way responsible for the spread and even that the virus might have originated with US military personnel were outlandish and the worst kind of propaganda we see from China. Others have criticized China for not releasing the best, most accurate current data about the virus and illness and deaths in China. Even worse, Tedros publicly accused Taiwanese of launching racist and discriminatory attacks against him and even threatening to hurt him. These remarks were largely denounced worldwide, and President Tsai Ing-wen strongly rebutted them and invited Tedros to Taiwan to see the excellent job the country had done controlling the virus. During a video interview with Radio Television Hong Kong's Yvonne Tong (唐若韞) on March 18, WHO Assistant Director-General Bruce Aylward claimed not to have heard a question on whether the WHO would consider giving Taiwan membership, then said that "all areas of China" had done a good job, and later cut the interview short. US Senator Rick Scott criticized the WHO for rejecting Taiwan's participation in the global body. "This is shameful. @WHO refuses to answer a basic question about #Taiwan, who they've refused to allow into the organization. More and more, the WHO seems to be a pawn of the Chinese Communist Party, which is very dangerous for world health," Scott said, and his comments were followed by similar statements from US Senator Marco Rubio. I would not disagree (*Taipei Times*, March 31, 2020; above art by Unsplash). In April, former US Ambassador to the United Nations Nikki Haley launched an online petition recommending the US Congress to probe whether China had covered up the coronavirus outbreak and to support Taiwan joining the WHO. Australia had also launched a drive for the WHO to investigate the origin and spread of the virus, which, not surprisingly, Chinese diplomatic personnel denounced.

I commented on the coronavirus, its impact in Taiwan and around the world, reactions, and Taiwan's role and behavior during the crisis, in the *Taipei Times* on April 14, 2020. I think a strength of this editorial is how I name the everyday activities that everyone is involved with in fighting the virus. This reached readers. As well, when I noted that we need not start a quarrel at this time with the WHO and others, and that more important work remains to be done, this was an important point. I also refer to the small outbreak that occurred in Taiwan when a navy vessel returned home, and it was found that the virus was widespread in the boat. This was a crucial issue in Taiwan for a number of weeks, but was brought under control.

Solidarity Worldwide Crucial at This Time

The COVID-19 pandemic has certainly disrupted life worldwide and descended on humanity like a curse from above, a devilish and deadly disease, seemingly an act of homicide against men and women everywhere.

It has introduced fear, dread, and anxiety into life in ways we could not have imagined only months ago and disrupted the normal process of life in incredible ways.

Only months ago I was not wearing a mask every moment out of doors, scrubbing my hands dozens of times a day, mopping with bleach solutions inside and outside my home, polishing doorknobs with anti-bacterial wipes, keeping 2 m and more distance between myself and others, and risking condemnation if I did not do all of these things.

Life has changed, apparently permanently, and in no way for the better.

What disturbs almost as much is how the comments on this disease by the worried masses are often extremely negative and exasperated (understandably), outwardly biased, or simply politicized in extreme ways.

Such extremism seems to be the likelihood in times like these, and yes, we must understand how people feel, but that does not excuse obstinate, jaundiced, and antagonizing attacks.

Probably here I should mention WHO Director-General Tedros Adhanom Ghebreyesus' recent attacks on Taiwan, which veered into the baseless and unfounded and were in sum denounced worldwide.

I appreciated President Tsai Ing-wen's (蔡英文) response to this on Facebook. No country should be "attacked" at a time like this, and the simple fact is that as emotions run high, we must control our responses.

Also over-politicized is the approach to China as the source of the virus and Taiwan's lack of a role in the WHO and its associated assemblies.

While China can and perhaps must be criticized for its role in all of this, at the same time, we must control our reactions and extend a humanitarian hand of assistance.

After all, China has also suffered during all of this. I denounce those who wish ill on China as a result of this disaster.

Nor is this the time to be hooting for Taiwan's inclusion in the WHO and any and all other groups Taiwan is excluded from. By its example so far during the crisis, Taiwan has been recognized globally and made a great contribution to humankind.

I do not endorse the exclusion of Taiwan from the WHO and other collectives, but now is not the time for bureaucratic, jurisdictional rambling and skirmishing.

This turns this issue into a standard policy argument that is commonly made in normal political times, but should be avoided in an emergency. That which is municipal, national, political, or communal should be dealt with in these times coincidentally, conjointly, and collectively, in the best ways we can.

We should avoid notions of "sovereignty," "self-determining," "autonomy," "populist," and the like during this emergency.

Although China's actions and behavior have been difficult and often unwarranted in terms of this crisis, now is not the time to launch a quarrel. There is too much else we must address.

In spite of all I say here, there have been constructive and helpful comments about how we must move ahead.

EU Commissioner for Crisis Management Janez Lenarcic said recently that "coordination and cooperation need to be our main focus. Now is the time to join forces in order to stop this epidemic. It is crucial that the entire international community focus on preparedness and response efforts to fight coronavirus, keeping international solidarity in mind."

These are the comments we must pay attention to.

I ran another piece in the *Taipei Times* on May 1, 2020. In this work I look at the COVID outbreak from more of a "political" angle, addressing the issues of freedom, order, and equality (core political values of different parties) and how these are playing out in terms of the protests against lockdowns, quarantines, and other protective measures in the country. I endorse order in society and how that can lead to improved conditions and control of this crisis.

Outbreaks Need Order, Not Protests

Like everyone else worldwide, the COVID-19 pandemic remains at the top of my concerns.

The virus has lashed out in devastating ways in countries everywhere and even Taiwan, recognized for its effective control of the disease, has been shaken.

Actions taking place are giving rise to new thoughts and apprehensions about this pandemic. I am referring first and foremost to demonstrations that have broken out in the United States, at which citizens have demanded to be freed from lockdowns, home stays, and quarantines, often roving streets and capitals without masks and other protective gear and openly flouting social distancing and other necessary safeguards and precautions.

In such actions, I see a particular angle on the concept of citizenship in (usually) democratic nations.

My point revolves around two main concepts and obligations of political and civic participation (and to some extent a third). I am referring to the concepts of "freedom" and "order" in society, along with "equality" (the third of my assumptions).

These ideas are at the core of how citizens view their role and aspirations in a polity.

How people consider and apply these points in their lives, and the given fidelities and allegiances they create in their (political) worldview, largely determine their political views—and here I generally mean conservative, liberal, communitarian, or libertarian.

We are seeing these intimations at play in the United States and elsewhere, in terms of these demonstrations.

Rallies have taken place across the United States, from a few dozen protesters in Virginia and Oregon to thousands in Michigan and Washington state.

The demonstrators are said to be conservative, pro-US president Donald Trump, pro-gun advocates (conservatives and libertarians, for the most part).

Many demonstrations have been said to be reminiscent of pro-Trump campaign events, with banners, T-shirts, and signs.

Assuming that this pro-conservative slant is true, we are seeing people exercising what they feel to be a right that they possess in society—the right to freely express themselves and meet openly against government regulations. Such "freedom" is a core value in the conservative pantheon.

To return to my points above, "order" is also a conservative value, but these demonstrators are choosing to contravene the focus on order so that they can exercise their freedom.

I find myself siding against these protesters and, instead, approving of "order" in society—in this case, the order imposed by governments and expected by others that requires people to stay at home, wear masks, maintain social distancing, and otherwise align themselves with broader expectations and demands.

This goes against my core values as a liberal, as we do not emphasize order in our politics.

An acquaintance of mine told me: "I would not have expected this of you."

The media have reported that demonstrations have flared in a number of countries, but the focus has been on those in the United States and their conservative elements.

This is the familiar melody of "fighting for freedom" that has long boiled in the veins of these people. You do not see this as prominently in many other countries, but it runs in the blood of many conservative and libertarian Americans.

A similar view popped up in Taiwan's virus emergency when a group of navy personnel were identified as having COVID-19, but they had for some time made their way across the nation and might have spread the coronavirus much more widely than has so far been determined.

Some of these sailors were identified and their destinations made public—and these destinations even included motels and hotels where they might have been meeting lovers.

The acquaintance I mentioned above stated strongly: "We are being watched and making these destinations public is wrong."

I disagreed, saying that the sailors having openly visited the destinations made it public information.

When you sign your name at a hotel, or use a credit card, that is public information. Yes, there are questions of privacy, with differing opinions, but the information is needed—all of this complies with my endorsement of order in a virus-stricken nation.

The concept of "equality" was noted above, but I am not sure that it fits neatly into this argument, except perhaps to say that we are all equally threatened by the coronavirus and must treat each other as equal "brothers in arms" during this difficulty.

Keep order in your communities, and cooperate with other citizens and the government—this is the best way to fend off this pandemic.

All the way into September, the virus is loose, and I can only hope for the best for all in the coming months and wish my readers safety and wellness. Let us pray that some good can emerge from all of this. Disaster has struck; now we must pull together and all help one another. Good luck now and always.

CHAPTER 9

Conclusion

To be sure, life in Taiwan has been good for even simpler reasons than all of the above. That is, I have simply liked it here on a personal level. I have expressed this in my *Something Super* memoir, which readers may find informative and yet more intimate in terms of the subjects we have examined in this book. I again point readers to this work for a very complete picture of life in Taiwan, from an expatriate's perspective. In *Something Super*, I expressed a simple feeling of just what Taiwan has given me, and I relate "my sometimes-agitated initiation into Taiwanese life and culture…my rich teaching life and experiences with students, my assiduous studies and attainment of a PhD, my memorable wedding, my further-agitated studies of the Chinese language, and comments on the heated politics and other issues in Taiwan" (these views may relate to this work). I add that "what has been great about Taiwan for me" is that, "although I have encountered my share of difficulties and trials since I moved here, I have…experienced a veritable wealth of good fortune, growth, and change. Taiwan has been good to me" (Fig. 9.1).

I concluded my memoir by reflecting on how my life in Taiwan had been "almost like some magical Chinese tale—maybe a Monkey King (孫悟空, sūnwùkōng) emerging from a mythical stone!—with transformation, something of a pilgrimage, travels to new worlds, and experiences with new languages and cultures. I may not have acquired supernatural powers, but something super has occurred to me in this land. Here in

D. Pendery, *Taiwan—A Light in the East*,
https://doi.org/10.1007/978-981-15-5604-3_9

Fig. 9.1 Taipei morning-scape

Taiwan, I have learned so much about others and myself, and I thank the people who have helped me, befriended me, and loved me."

The above may seem somewhat "personal," but as I stated at the beginning of this book, it is both a personal and analytical examination. And even the above can be seen as "political"—a look into the heart and mind of Taiwan, the nation. This sums up all that I feel about this democratic, free, and for me, loving nation.

This concludes my book examining Taiwan's life, history, culture, politics, education, identity, aesthetics, and future. As I have said, although there are some personal touches, my aim in this work was not an individual memoir, but an analytical, investigative look at Taiwan's life and civic heart. I hope that I have been successful in this respect and that I have expressed in expository, inquiring ways the new actualities that have constantly surprised me in Taiwan. Above all, I hope I have shared the wonders that have charmed and fascinated me, tickled my imagination, and challenged my beliefs, views, and prospects for going on 20 years.

The expressions and examinations that I have presented in this work, the majority published in the English-language newspaper, *Taipei Times*, represent a new facet of my life. I have thought about the years I lived in the United States in San Francisco and Boston, and I realize that although these are very "political" cities, in fact I never contributed in any way to the civic dialog that was taking place. That is, I never wrote a single letter to the editor, much less wrote an editorial for publication during that time (this was something of a slow period in my writing life). In Taiwan, it started the same way, but that changed in about 2006, when I published the first of dozens of letters that the *Taipei Times* would publish, and 2008, when my first editorial appeared. As this progressed, I realized that I had "found my voice" in Taiwan—to be sure an unexpected development in Asia, far from my original home! I am extremely happy to have found this outlet, this channel for my views and expression, and I am proud and happy that I have indeed contributed to the social conversation in Taiwan. I should thank the editors at the *Taipei Times*, particularly, for giving me so much opportunity in their publication. I would also like to thank Professor Damm for his generous assistance (Fig. 9.2).

Fig. 9.2 Temple arch

As I look ahead, my hope is that I can see and meet new people and friends in Taiwan for a long time to come. After my discussion of future possibilities in Taiwan above, my own future in Taiwan seems fairly set in stone. I have stated and implied that I do not intend to return to my home in the United States, and I suspect I will die and be laid to rest in this island nation, and that is something I will never regret. I am an "Asian" now old friends and family, and my hope is that you can join me in this enthralling new adventure. My best to all the good people I have known in Taiwan and all around the world, and I look forward to greeting you here soon!

Year 2020, the Chinese year of the rat—is also my birth year. Readers may know that according to the Chinese zodiac, in the race held by the Jade Emperor to choose the zodiac animals, the astute rat asked the hard-working ox to take him on a ride behind its ear to cross the river. The rat thus won the race and became the first of the zodiac animals. It pains me that this year of the rat is looking to be anything but so promising. My hopes and prayers go out to all around the world as we tackle this crisis, and I hope we emerge at the "finish line" healthy and happy.

Sources Cited[1,2]

Books and Academic Journals Cited Include:

Acemoglu, Daron, James A. Robinson (2019). *The Narrow Corridor: Sates, Societies, and the Fate of Liberty*. Penguin Press.

Albert, Lothar Brock, Klaus Dieter Wolf, eds. (2000). *Civilizing World Politics: Society and Community Beyond the State*, Rowman & Littlefield Publishers. On the Internet at https://books.google.com.tw/books.

Baldwin, David A. (1980). "Interdependence and Power: A Conceptual Analysis," International Organization, Vol. 34, No. 4, pp. 471–506. University of Wisconsin Press.

Bush, Richard, Ryan Hass (n.d.). "Taiwan's democracy and the China challenge," Foreign Policy at Brookings. On the Internet at https://www.brookings.edu/wp-content/uploads/2018/12/FP_20190226_taiwan_bush_hass.pdf.

Chen, Piera, Dinah Gardner (2017). *Lonely Planet, Taiwan*. On the Internet at https://books.google.com.tw/books.

[1] A number of media sources were used in this book, including newspapers, certain Internet locations, magazines, etc. These included *The International Journal of Taiwan Studies, Taipei Times, Taiwan News, Wikipedia, Global Firepower, Up News Info, Nikkei Asian Review, New York Times, Newsweek, Up News Info, Science Daily, Kyodo News, The Straits Times, NTUBulletin, Times' Thunderer*, the *Kuomintang Official Website, Taiwan.gov.tw, Quarts, Reuters, BBC History Magazine, Foreign Policy*, the World Bank, the *Taiwan President's Office*, the *Taiwan Ministry of Education* and *Times Higher Education*.

[2] Note that the *Taipei Times* has informed me that I hold all rights to my work published in the newspaper.

D. Pendery, *Taiwan—A Light in the East*,
https://doi.org/10.1007/978-981-15-5604-3

Cohen, Mitchell (ed.) (2018). *Princeton Readings in Political Thought: Essential Texts since Plato*, Princeton University Press. On the Internet at https://books.google.com.tw/.

Damm, Jens (2011a). "Taiwan's Ethnicities and their Representation on the Internet," in *Journal of Current Chinese Affairs*, March, 2011, 40 (1), 99–131. On the Internet at https://journals.sagepub.com/doi/full/10.1177/186810261104000104.

——— (2012). "The Multiculturalization of Taiwan: From a Unified Han-Identity to the 'Four Great Ethnic Groups.'" In *The Globalization of Confucius and Confucianism (Chinese History and Society/Berliner China-Hefte)*, Klaus Muhlhahn, Nathalie van Looy (eds.) 72–89. LIT Verlag.

——— (2011b). "From 'Overseas Chinese' to 'Overseas Taiwanese': Questions of Identity and Belonging in the Cyberspace," Gunter Schubert, Jens Damm (eds.). 218–236. Routledge.

Diamond, Jared (2019). *Upheaval: How Nations Cope with Crisis and Change*, Little Brown and Co. Little, Brown and Co. Penguin Books.

——— (2005). *Collapse: How Societies Choose to Fail or Succeed*, Penguin Books.

Hsin-Huang Michael Hsiao (2019). "My Journey of Social Movements and Civil Society Research Revisited," in Fell, Dafydd, Michael Hsiao (eds.). *Taiwan Studies Revisited*, Routledge Research on Taiwan Series, 1st Edition. On the Internet at https://books.google.com.tw/books.

Jacobs, Bruce (2019). "The Rise of the Dutch Empire: The Broader Context of the Dutch Colonisation of Taiwan," *International Journal of Taiwan Studies*, Volume 2, Issue 2, September 2019, 365–375. On the Internet at https://www.researchgate.net/.

Jacques, Martin (2009). *When China Rules the World: The Rise of the Middle Kingdom and the End of the Western World*, Allen Lane, an imprint of Penguin Books.

Parrado, Nando, with Vince Rause, 2006. *Miracle in the Andes*, Crown Publishers.

Paul, T.V. (2010). *South Asia's Weak States Understanding the Regional Insecurity Predicament*, Stanford University Press.

Pence, Mike (2019). "Remarks by Vice President Pence at the Frederic V. Malek Memorial Lecture." On the Internet at https://www.whitehouse.gov/briefings-statements/remarks-vice-president-pence-frederic-v-malek-memorial-lecture/.

Pendery, David (2013). *Something Super: Living, Learning and Teaching in Taiwan*, Lynx Publishing.

Rigger, Shelley (2011). *Why Taiwan Matters: Small Island, Global Powerhouse*, Rowman & Littlefield Publishers.

Rosen, Stephen Peter (1990). *Innovation and the Modern Military: Winning the Next War*. Cornell University Press.

Schubert, Gunter, editor (2015). *Taiwan and the 'China Impact': Challenges and Opportunities*, Routledge, Research on Taiwan Series.

St. Augustine, Confessions: The Works of St. Augustine, a Translation for the 21st Century. Introduction, translation and notes by Maria Boulding, John E. Rotelle, ed. New City Press, New York, 1997.

Story, Joseph (1851). *Commentaries on the U.S. Constitution, A Preliminary Review.* Originally published by C.C. Little and J. Brown, Boston. On the Internet at https://books.google.com.tw/books.

Templeman, Kharis (2019). "Blessings in Disguise: How Authoritarian Legacies and the China Factor Have Strengthened Democracy in Taiwan." *International Journal of Taiwan Studies,* Volume 2, Issue 2, September 2019, 230–263. On the Internet at https://www.researchgate.net/.

Tsai, Ing-wen (2019). "President Tsai delivers 2019 National Day Address." On the Internet at https://english.president.gov.tw/News/5869.

Wang, Li-jung (王俐容) (2007). "Diaspora, Identity and Cultural Citizenship: The Hakkas in 'Multicultural Taiwan,'" Ethnic and Racial Studies, 30, 5, 875–895. On the Internet at http://www.srcs.nctu.edu.tw/speech_pages/CSA2005/papers/0108_C3_3_Wang.pdf.

Welton, Michael (2019). "Two Theories of Democracy, Counterpunch." On the Internet at https://www.counterpunch.org/2019/11/01/two-theories-of-democracy/.

Index[1]

[1] Note: Page numbers followed by 'n' refer to notes.

D. Pendery, *Taiwan—A Light in the East*,
https://doi.org/10.1007/978-981-15-5604-3

The manufacturer's authorised representative in the EU is Springer Nature Customer Service Centre GmbH, Europaplatz 3, 69115 Heidelberg, Germany. If you have any concerns regarding our products, please contact ProductSafety@springernature.com

Printed and bound by CPI Group (UK) Ltd, Croydon, CR0 4YY
25/09/2026
02222903-0001